A-Z ROMFORD and ILFORD

CONTEN

REFERENCE

Motorway	**M25**	Car Park (selected)	P
A Road	A12	Church or Chapel	†
B Road	B177	Fire Station	■
Dual Carriageway		Hospital	H
One-way Street	→	House Numbers (A & B Roads only)	13 / 8
Traffic flow on A roads is indicated by a heavy line on the driver's left.		Information Centre	i
Junction Name	MOBY DICK	National Grid Reference	⁵50
Restricted Access		Police Station	▲
Pedestrianized Road		Post Office	★
Track & Footpath		Toilet:	
Residential Walkway		without facilities for the Disabled	▽
		with facilities for the Disabled	▽
Railway Stations:	Tunnel / Level Crossing	Disabled facilities only	▽
National Rail Network		Educational Establishment	
Underground	●	Hospital or Hospice	
Built-up Area	OLIVE / AV.	Industrial Building	
Local Authority Boundary		Leisure or Recreational Facility	
Posttown Boundary		Place of Interest	
Postcode Boundary (within posttown)		Public Building	
Map Continuation	12	Shopping Centre or Market	
		Other Selected Buildings	

SCALE

1:15,840				¾ Mile	6.31 cm to 1 km
4 inches to 1 mile	0 ¼ ½				10.16 cm to 1 mile
	0 250 500 750 1 Kilometre				

Copyright of Geographers' A-Z Map Company Limited

Head Office:
Fairfield Road, Borough Green, Sevenoaks, Kent TN15 8PP
Telephone: 01732 781000 (Enquiries & Trade Sales)
01732 783422 (Retail Sales)

www.a-zmaps.co.uk

Copyright © Geographers' A-Z Map Co. Ltd.

Edition 2 2005

Ordnance Survey®

This product includes mapping data licensed from Ordnance Survey® with the permission of the Controller of Her Majesty's Stationery Office.

G000293570

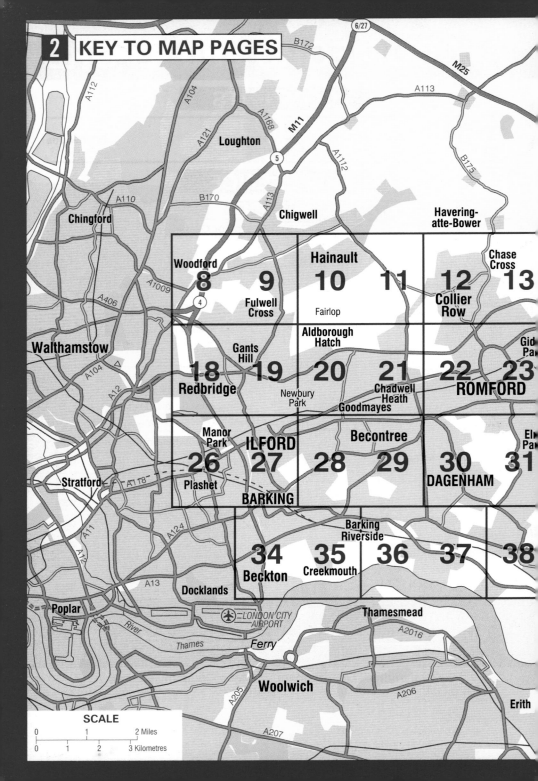

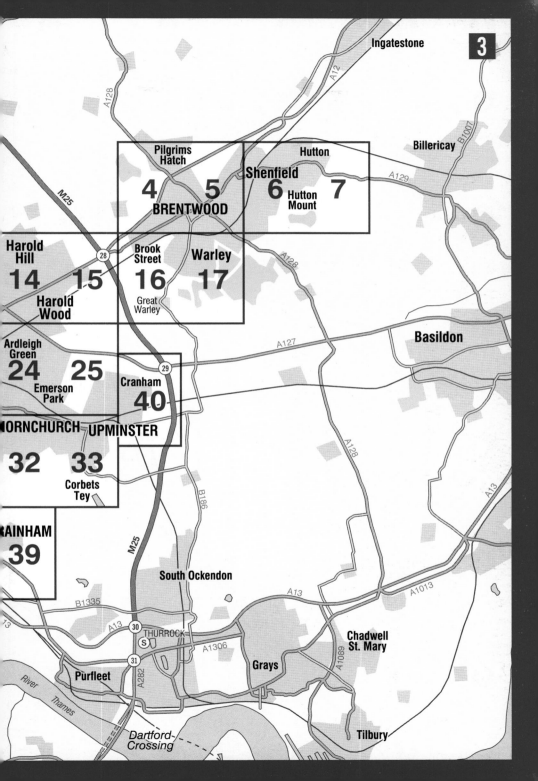

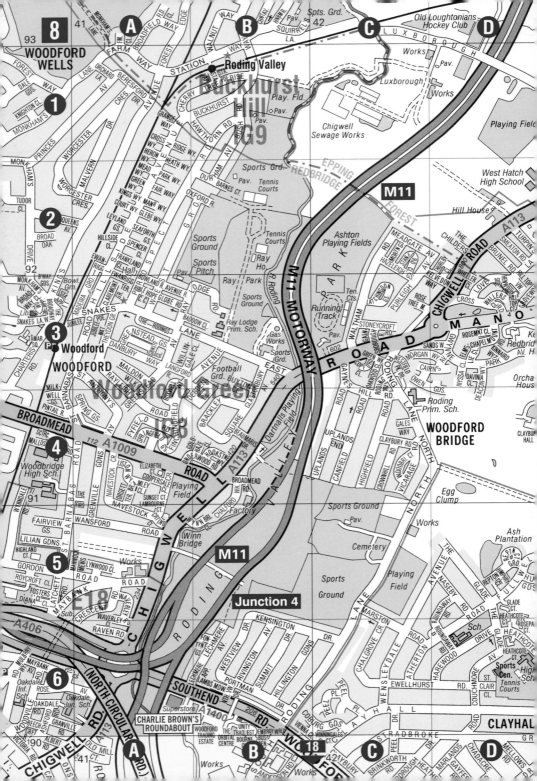

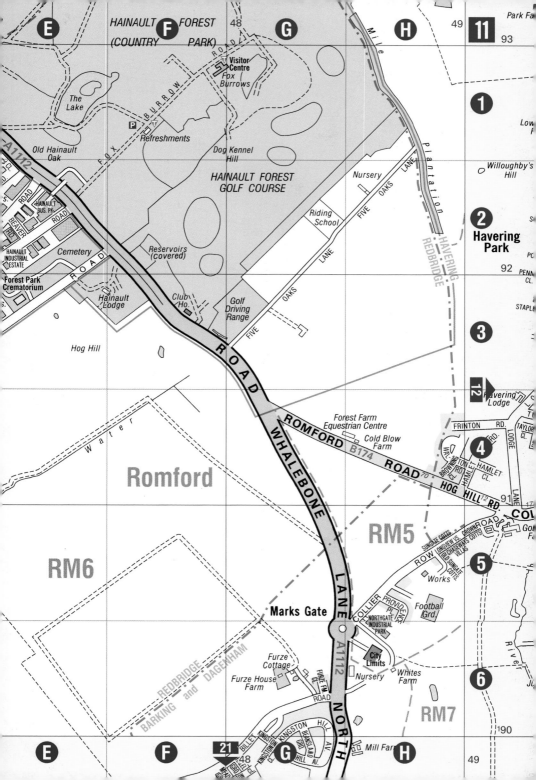

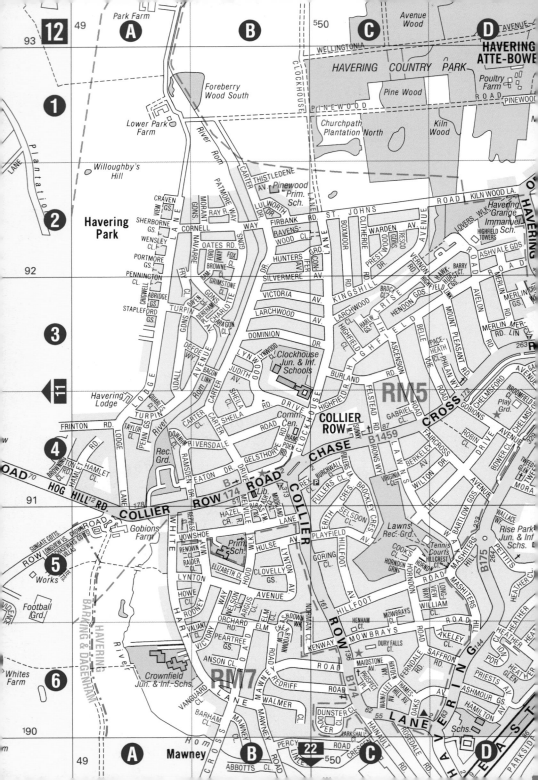

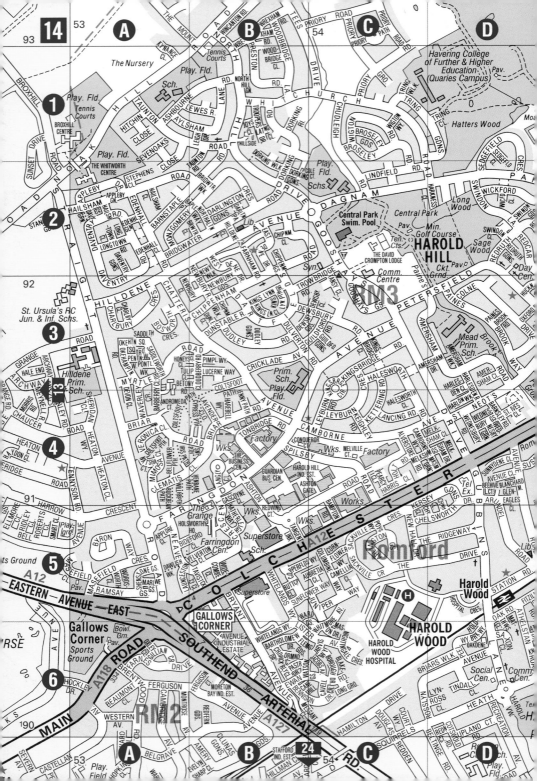

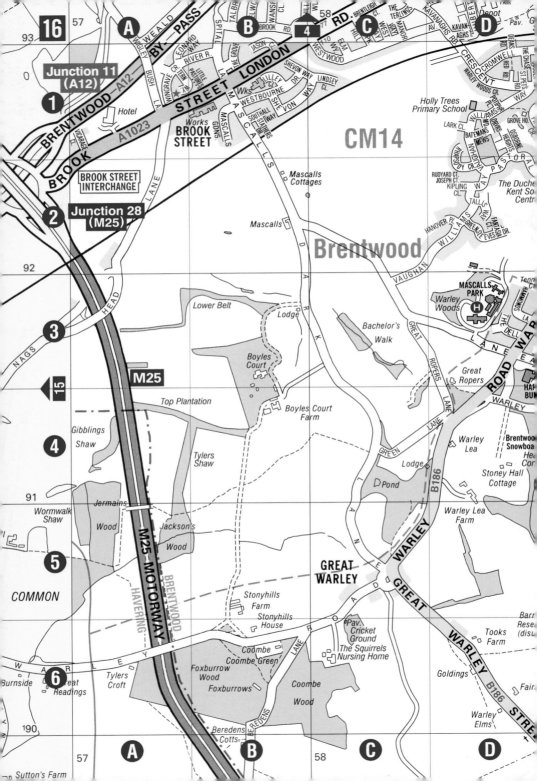

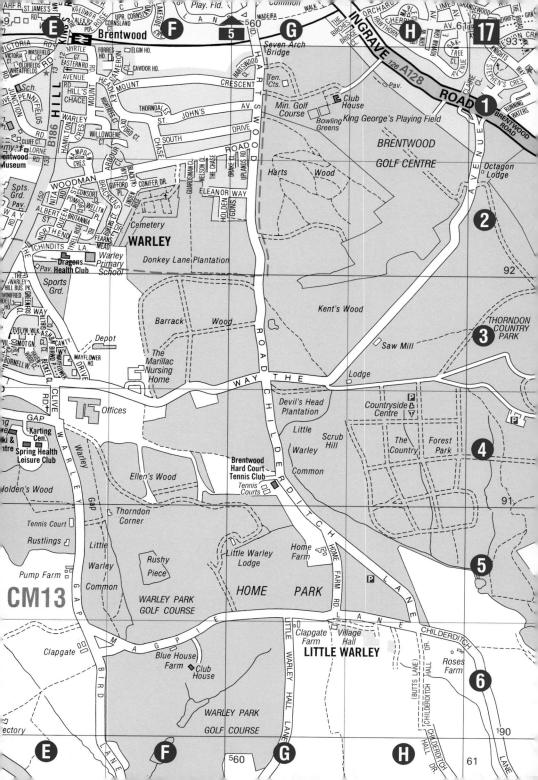

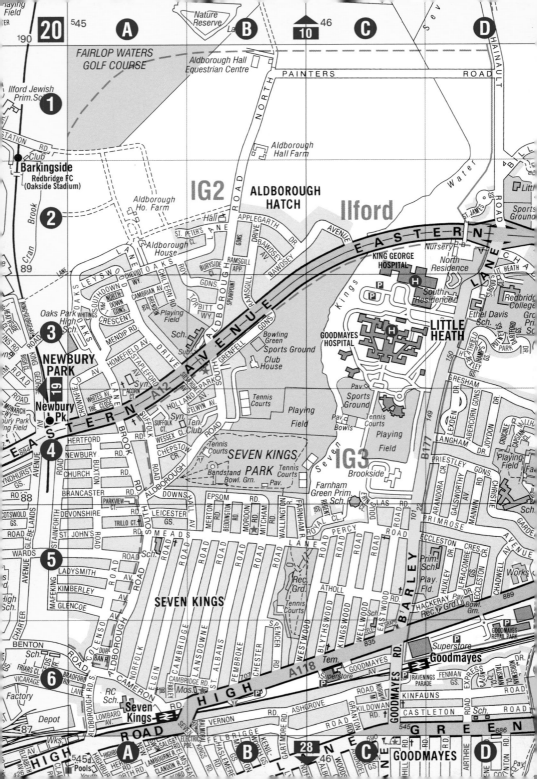

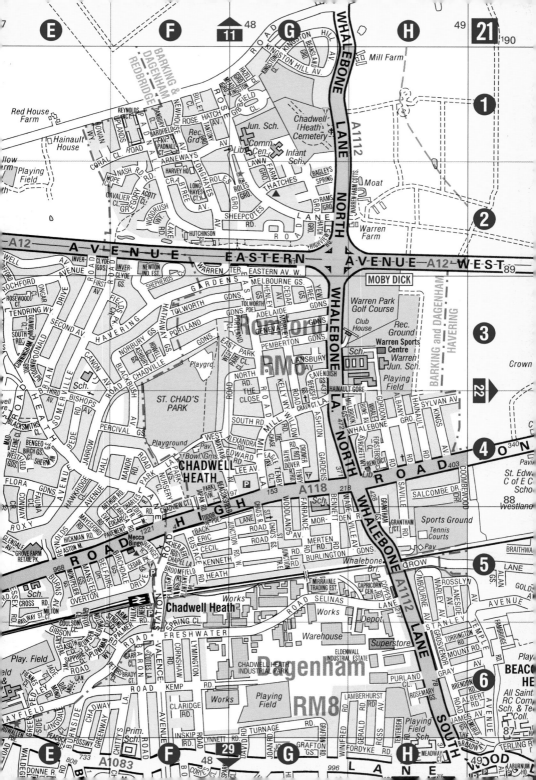

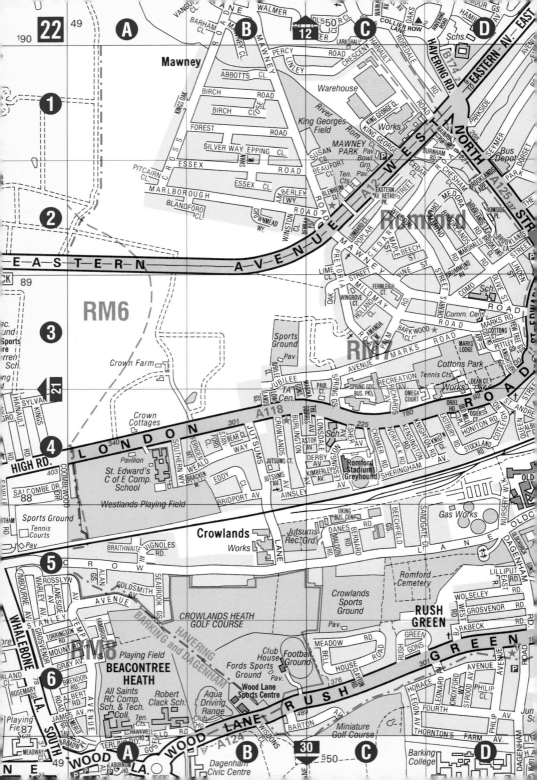

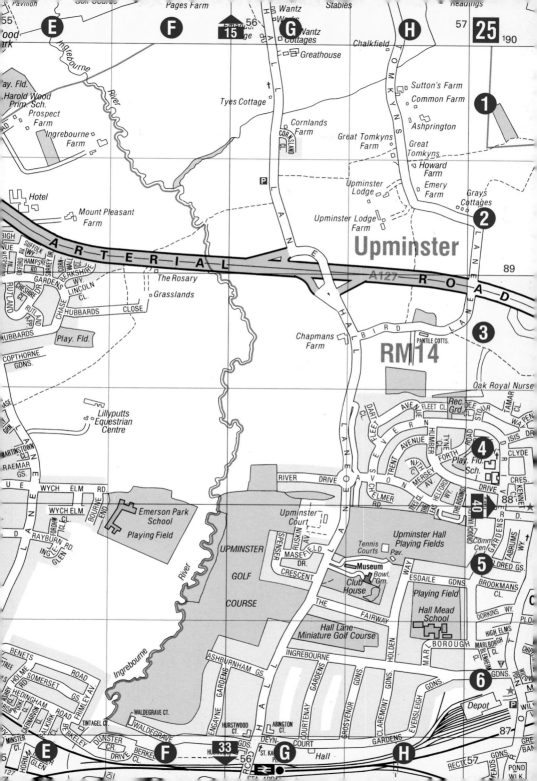

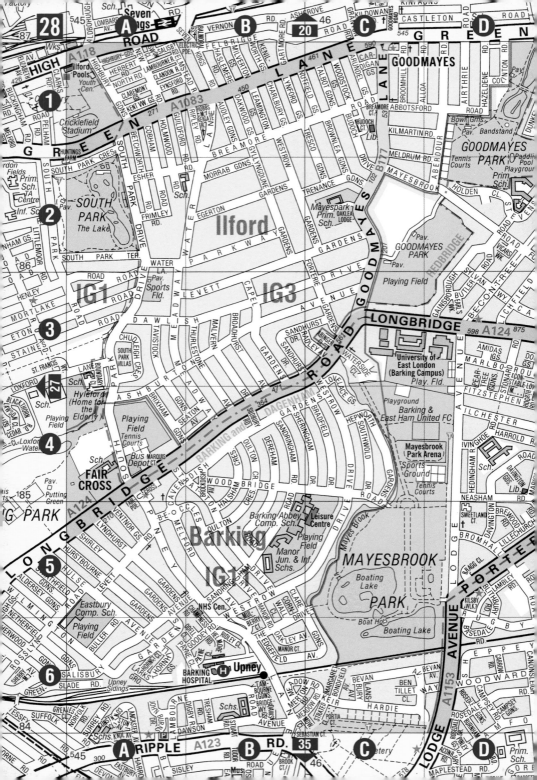

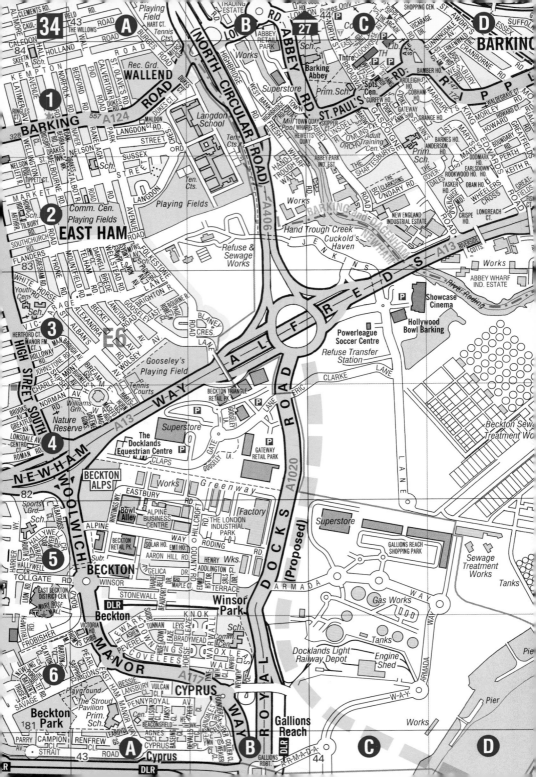

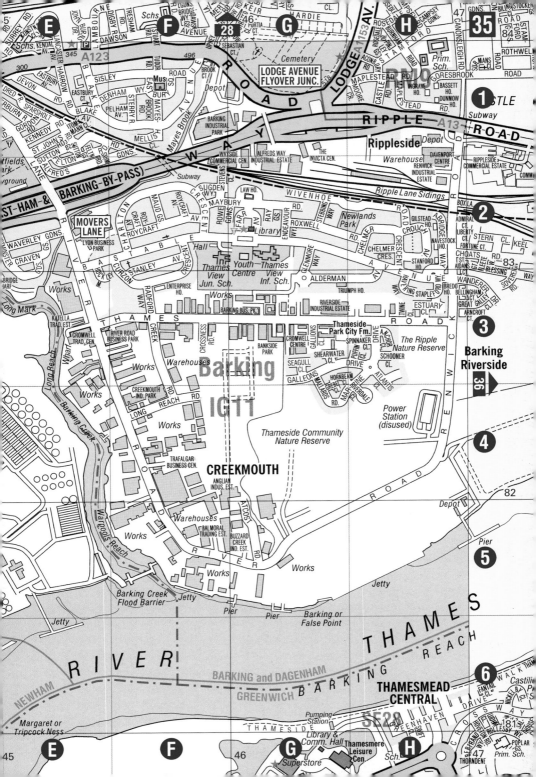

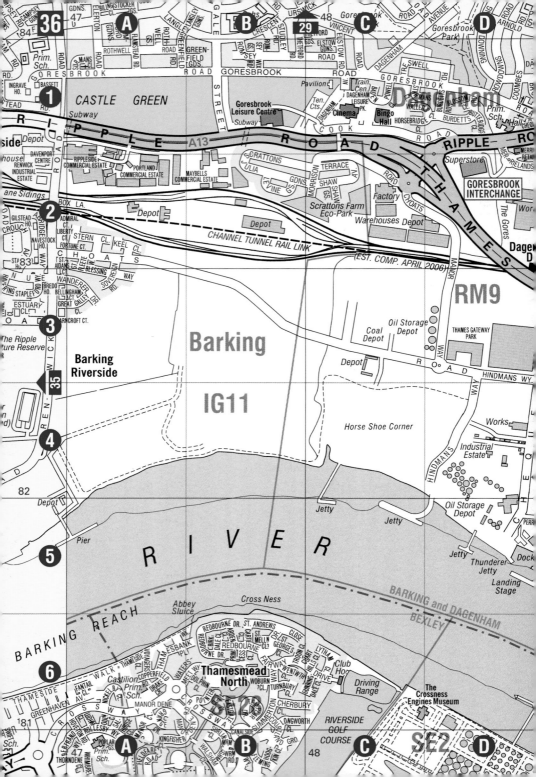

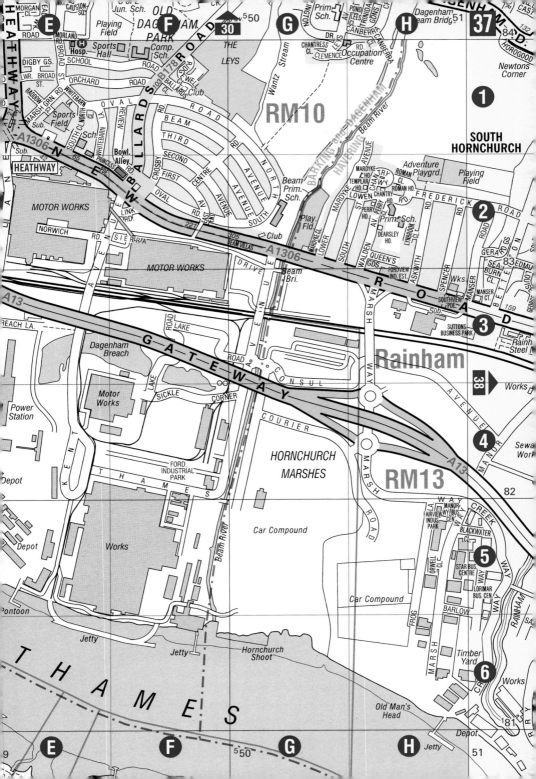

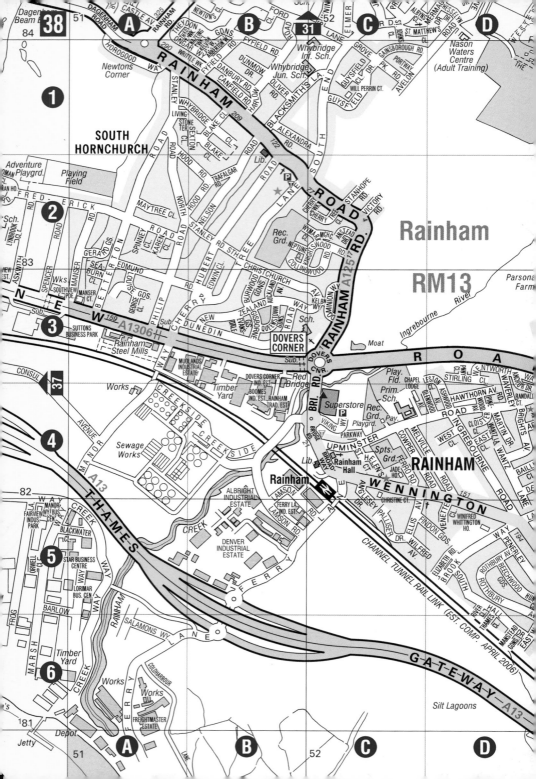

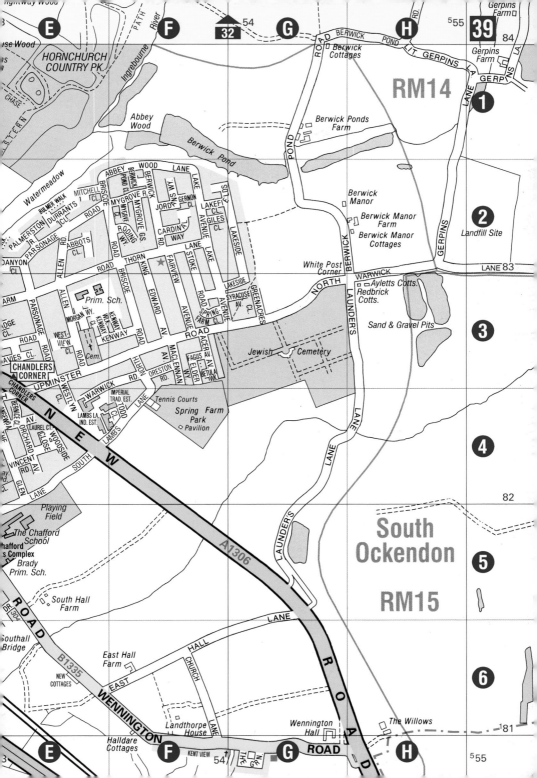

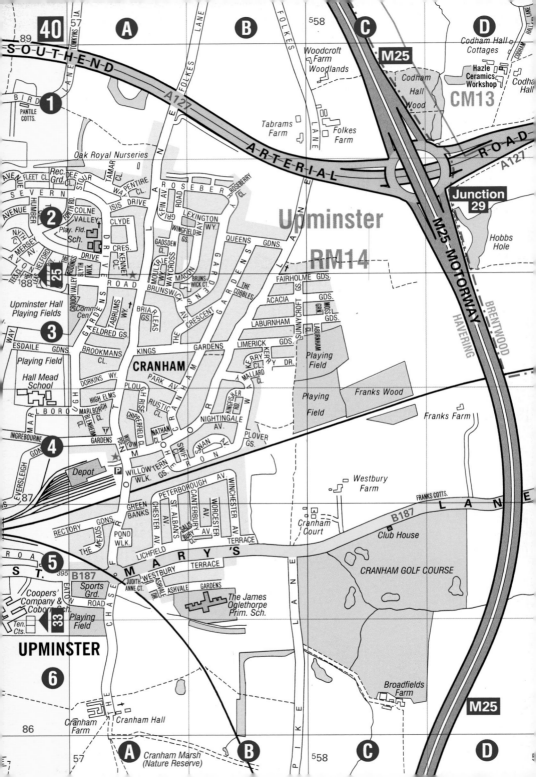

INDEX

Including Streets, Places & Areas, Hospitals & Hospices, Industrial Estates,
Selected Flats & Walkways, Junction Names, Stations, and Selected Places of Interest.

HOW TO USE THIS INDEX

1. Each street name is followed by its Postcode District (or, if outside the London Postcodes, by its Locality Abbreviation(s)), and then by its map reference;
e.g. **Aaron Hill Rd.** E6: Lon . . . .5A **34** is in the E6 Postcode District and is to be found in square 5A on page **34**. The page number being shown in bold type.

2. A strict alphabetical order is followed in which Av., Rd., St., etc. (though abbreviated) are read in full and as part of the street name;
e.g. **Apple Ga.** appears after **Applegarth Dr.** but before **Appleton Way**

3. Streets and a selection of flats and walkways too small to be shown on the maps, appear in the index with the thoroughfare to which it is connected shown
in brackets; e.g. **Abbots Ct.** RM3: Hrld W . . . .5D **14** (off Queen's Pk. Rd.)

4. Addresses that are in more than one part are referred to as not continuous.

5. Places and areas are shown in the index in **BLUE TYPE** and the map reference is to the actual map square in which the town centre or area is located and not to the
place name shown on the map; e.g. BARKING 6G 27

6. An example of a selected place of interest is Brentwood Mus. 1E 17

7. An example of a station is Barkingside Station (Tube) 1H 19

8. Junction names are shown in the index in **BOLD CAPITAL TYPE**; e.g. **BECKTON ALPS** 4A 34

9. An example of a hospital is BARKING HOSPITAL 6B 28

GENERAL ABBREVIATIONS

App. : Approach	**Dr.** : Drive	**La.** : Lane	**Rdbt.** : Roundabout
Arc. : Arcade	**E.** : East	**Lit.** : Little	**Shop.** : Shopping
Av. : Avenue	**Ent.** : Enterprise	**Lwr.** : Lower	**Sth.** : South
Blvd. : Boulevard	**Est.** : Estate	**Mnr.** : Manor	**Sq.** : Square
Bri. : Bridge	**Fld.** : Field	**Mans.** : Mansions	**St.** : Street
B'way. : Broadway	**Flds.** : Fields	**Mkt.** : Market	**Ter.** : Terrace
Bus. : Business	**Gdns.** : Gardens	**Mdw.** : Meadow	**Twr.** : Tower
Cvn. : Caravan	**Ga.** : Gate	**Mdws.** : Meadows	**Trad.** : Trading
Cen. : Centre	**Gt.** : Great	**M.** : Mews	**Up.** : Upper
Cir. : Circus	**Grn.** : Green	**Mt.** : Mount	**Vw.** : View
Cl. : Close	**Gro.** : Grove	**Mus.** : Museum	**Vs.** : Villas
Cnr. : Corner	**Hgts.** : Heights	**Nth.** : North	**Vis.** : Visitors
Cott. : Cottage	**Ho.** : House	**Pde.** : Parade	**Wlk.** : Walk
Cotts. : Cottages	**Ho's.** : Houses	**Pk.** : Park	**W.** : West
Ct. : Court	**Ind.** : Industrial	**Pl.** : Place	**Yd.** : Yard
Cres. : Crescent	**Info.** : Information	**Ri.** : Rise	
Cft. : Croft	**Junc.** : Junction	**Rd.** : Road	

LOCALITY ABBREVIATIONS

Avel : **Aveley**	Gt War : **Great Warley**	L Bur : **Little Burstead**	Shenf : **Shenfield**
Bark : **Barking**	Hrld W : **Harold Wood**	L War : **Little Warley**	S Weald : **South Weald**
Bwood : **Brentwood**	Have B : **Havering-Atte-Bower**	Mawney : **Mawney**	Upm : **Upminster**
Buck H : **Buckhurst Hill**	Heron : **Herongate**	Mount : **Mountnessing**	War : **Warley**
Chad H : **Chadwell Heath**	Horn : **Hornchurch**	Pil H : **Pilgrims Hatch**	Wenn : **Wennington**
Chig : **Chigwell**	Hut : **Hutton**	Rain : **Rainham**	Wfd G : **Woodford Green**
Col R : **Collier Row**	Ilf : **Ilford**	Rom : **Romford**	
Dag : **Dagenham**	Ingve : **Ingrave**	Rush G : **Rush Green**	

A

Aaron Hill Rd. E6: Lon 5A **34**
Abberton Wlk. RM13: Rain 1B **38**
Abbey Cl. RM1: Rom 4G **23**
Abbey Pk. Ind. Est.
    IG11: Bark 2C **34**
Abbey Retail Pk. IG11: Bark 6F **27**
Abbey Rd. IG2: Ilf 3H **19**
    IG11: Bark 1B **34**
Abbey Sports Cen. 1C **34**
Abbey Wharf Ind. Est.
    IG11: Bark 3D **34**
Abbey Wood La. RM13: Rain 2F **39**
Abbots Cl. CM15: Shenf 4A **6**
    RM13: Rain 2F **39**
Abbots Ct. RM3: Hrld W 5D **14**
    (off Queen's Pk. Rd.)
Abbotsford Rd. IG3: Ilf 1C **28**
Abbotswood Gdns. IG5: Ilf 1D **18**
Abbotts Cl. RM7: Mawney 1B **22**
Abbs Cross RM12: Horn 6A **24**
Abbs Cross Gdns.
    RM12: Horn 6A **24**
Abbs Cross La. RM12: Horn 2A **32**
Abenberg Way CM13: Hut 5B **6**
Abercorn Rd. RM6: Chad H 4D **20**
Aberdour Rd. IG3: Ilf 2D **28**
Abigail M. RM3: Hrld W 6D **14**
Abinger Cl. IG11: Bark 3C **28**

Abington Ct. RM14: Upm 6G **25**
Abraham Ct. RM14: Upm 1E **33**
Abraham Fisher Ho. E12 . . . . . .4E **27**
Abridge Gdns. RM5: Col R 3A **12**
Abridge Way IG11: Bark 2H **35**
Acacia Av. RM12: Horn 1F **31**
Acacia Dr. RM14: Upm 3E **33**
Acacia Gdns. RM14: Upm 3B **40**
Academy Flds. Rd.
    RM2: Rom 3H **23**
Accrington Ho. RM3: Rom 2B **14**
    (off Montgomery Cres.)
Acer Av. RM13: Rain 3F **39**
Acle Cl. IG6: Ilf 4F **9**
Aconbury Rd. RM9: Dag 1H **35**
Acorn Cen., The IG6: Ilf 3D **10**
Acorn Ct. E6 . . . . .6C **26**
    IG2: Ilf 4A **20**
Acorns, The IG7: Chig 1A **10**
Acre Rd. RM10: Dag 6B **30**
Acre Vw. RM11: Horn 2C **24**
Addison Rd. IG6: Ilf 5G **9**
Adelaide Gdns. RM6: Chad H . .3G **21**
Adelaide Rd. IG1: Ilf 1F **27**
Adeliza Cl. IG11: Bark 6G **27**
Adelphi Cres. RM12: Horn 1G **31**
Aden Rd. IG1: Ilf 5G **19**
Admiral Cl. IG11: Bark 2H **35**
Admirals Cl. E18 . . . . .2A **18**
Admirals Ct. E6 . . . . .6B **34**
    (off Trader Rd.)

Admirals Lodge RM1: Rom 2F **23**
Adnams Wlk. RM13: Rain 5G **31**
Adomar Rd. RM8: Dag 2F **29**
Agister Rd. IG7: Chig 2C **10**
Agnes Av. IG1: Ilf 3E **27**
Agnes Cl. E6 . . . . .6A **34**
Agnes Gdns. RM8: Dag 3F **29**
Aidan Cl. RM8: Dag 3G **29**
Ainsley Av. RM7: Rom 4B **22**
Aintree Cres. IG6: Ilf 6G **9**
Aintree Gro. RM14: Upm 2D **32**
Airfield Pathway RM12: Horn . . .6A **32**
Airfield Way RM12: Horn 5H **31**
Airlie Gdns. IG1: Ilf 6F **19**
Airthrie Rd. IG3: Ilf 1D **28**
Alan Gdns. RM7: Rush G 5A **22**
Albany Rd. CM15: Pil H 2D **4**
    E12 . . . . .3B **26**
    RM6: Chad H 4H **21**
    RM12: Horn 6G **23**
Albatross Cl. E6 . . . . .5A **34**
Albemarle App. IG2: Ilf 4F **19**
Albemarle Gdns. IG2: Ilf 4F **19**
Albert Ho. E18 . . . . .1A **18**
    (off Albert Rd.)
Albert Rd. E18 . . . . .1A **18**
    IG1: Ilf 2F **27**
    RM1: Rom 3F **23**
    RM8: Dag 6A **22**
Albert St. CM14: War 2E **17**
Albion Cl. RM7: Rom 4D **22**

Albright Ind. Est. RM13: Rain . . .4B **38**
Albury M. E12 . . . . .1A **26**
Albyns Cl. RM13: Rain 6G **31**
Alcester Ho. RM3: Rom 2B **14**
    (off Northallerton Way)
Aldborough Ct. IG2: Ilf 3B **20**
    (off Aldborough Rd. Nth.)
ALDBOROUGH HATCH 2B **20**
Aldborough Rd. RM10: Dag 5C **30**
    RM14: Upm 1D **32**
Aldborough Rd. Nth. IG2: Ilf . . .3B **20**
Aldborough Rd. Sth. IG3: Ilf . . .6A **20**
    RM14: Upm 3D **32**
Aldergrove Wlk.
    RM12: Horn 5A **32**
Alderman Av. IG11: Bark 3G **35**
Alderman La. E12 . . . . .2D **26**
Aldersbrook La. E12 . . . . .1A **26**
Aldersbrook Rd. E12 . . . . .1A **26**
Aldersey Gdns. IG11: Bark 5H **27**
Alderton Cl. CM15: Pil H 1D **4**
Alder Wlk. IG1: Ilf 4G **27**
Aldingham Ct. RM12: Horn 4H **31**
    (off Easedale Dr.)
Aldingham Gdns.
    RM12: Horn 4G **31**
Aldington Cl. RM8: Dag 6E **21**
Aldwych Av. IG6: Ilf 2G **19**
Aldwych Cl. RM11: Horn 1G **31**
Alexander La. CM13: Hut 2B **6**
    CM15: Shenf 1A **6**
Alexandra Av. IG8: Ilf 4E **9**

Alexandra Rd.—Becket Av.

Alexandra Rd. CM14: Bwood 6E 5
E6 .3A 34
RM1: Rom 4F 23
RM6: Chad H 4G 21
RM13: Rain 1B 38
Alfred Ho. *E12 . . . . .6C 26*
(off Tennyson Av.)
Alfred Prior Ho. E12 . . . . .3E 27
Alfred Rd. CM14: Bwood 5F 5
Alfred's Gdns. IG11: Bark 2E 35
Alfreds Way IG11: Bark 3B 34
Alfreds Way Ind. Est.
IG11: Bark 1G 35
Alibon Gdns. RM10: Dag 4A 30
Alibon Rd. RM9: Dag 4H 29
RM10: Dag 4A 30
Alison Cl. E6 . . . . .6A 34
Allandale Rd. RM11: Horn 5F 23
Allenby Dr. RM11: Horn 6C 24
Allen Rd. RM13: Rain 2E 39
Alleyndale Rd. RM8: Dag 1E 29
Alloa Rd. IG3: Ilf 1C 28
Alma Av. RM12: Horn 3C 32
Alpha Rd. CM13: Hut 2D 6
Alpine Bus. Cen. E6 . . . . .5A 34
Alpine Way E6 . . . . .5A 34
Althorne Way RM10: Dag 1A 30
Altmore Av. E6 . . . . .6D 26
Alverstoke Rd. RM3: Rom 4C 14
Alverstone Rd. E12 . . . . .3E 27
Alwyne Av. CM15: Shenf 2A 6
Amanda Cl. IG7: Chig 3H 9
Amanda M. RM7: Rom 3C 22
Amber La. IG6: Ilf 4F 9
Amberley Way RM7: Mawney . . .2B 22
Ambleside Av. RM12: Horn 4H 31
Ambleside Gdns. IG4: Ilf 2C 18
Amersham Cl. RM3: Rom 3D 14
Amersham Dr. RM3: Rom 3C 14
Amersham Rd. RM3: Rom 3C 14
Amersham Wlk. RM3: Rom 3D 14
Amery Gdns. RM2: Rom 1B 24
Amesbury Rd. RM9: Dag 6F 29
Amidas Gdns. RM8: Dag 3D 28
Ampthill Ho. *RM3: Rom 2B 14*
(off Montgomery Cres.)
Amwell Vw. IG6: Chig, Ilf 2D 10
Anchor Cl. IG11: Bark 3H 35
Anchor Dr. RM13: Rain 3D 38
Anchor Rd. E12 . . . . .1B 26
Anderson Ho. IG11: Bark 1D 34
Anderson Rd. IG8: Wfd G 1B 18
Andrew Cl. IG6: Ilf 3H 9
Andromeda Ct. RM3: Rom 4A 14
Angelica Dr. E6 . . . . .5A 34
Angel Way RM1: Rom 3E 23
Angle Grn. RM8: Dag 6E 21
Anglesey Dr. RM13: Rain 4C 38
Anglia Ct. *RM8: Dag 6F 21*
(off Spring Cl.)
Anglian Ind. Est. IG11: Bark 4F 35
Anglia Wlk. *E6 . . . . .1A 34*
(off Napier Rd.)
Annan Way RM1: Rom 5E 13
Anne Nastri Ct. *RM2: Rom 3H 23*
(off Heath Pk. Rd.)
Anne Way IG6: Ilf 3G 9
Annie Taylor Ho. *E12 . . . . .3E 27*
(off Walton Rd.)
Anson Cl. RM7: Mawney 6B 12
Anstead Dr. RM13: Rain 2C 38
Apollo Cl. RM12: Horn 1H 31
Appleby Dr. RM3: Rom 2A 14
Appleby Grn. RM3: Rom 2A 14
Appledore Cl. RM3: Rom 5A 14
Applegarth Dr. IG2: Ilf 2B 20
Apple Ga. CM14: Pil H 1B 4
Appleton Way RM12: Horn 6B 24
Approach, The RM14: Upm 2F 33
Aragon Cl. RM5: Col R 3B 12
Aragon Ct. IG6: Ilf 4G 9
Aragon Dr. IG6: Ilf 4G 9
Arandora Cres. RM6: Chad H . . .5D 20
Arbour Cl. CM14: War 2E 17
Arbour Way RM12: Horn 4H 31
Arcade, The IG11: Bark 6G 27
RM3: Rom 2B 14
(off Farnham Rd.)
Arcade Pl. RM1: Rom 3E 23
Archibald Rd. RM3: Hrld W 5E 15
Archway RM3: Rom 3H 13
Arden Cl. SE28 . . . . .6B 36
Arden Cres. RM9: Dag 6E 29
Ardleigh Cl. RM11: Horn 1B 24
Ardleigh Ct. CM15: Shenf 3H 5
Ardleigh Gdns. CM13: Hut 2E 7
ARDLEIGH GREEN 2A 24
Ardleigh Grn. Rd.
RM11: Horn 3B 24
Ardleigh Ho. IG11: Bark 1C 34
Ardleigh M. IG1: Ilf 2F 27
Ardwell Av. IG6: Ilf 3G 19
Argus Cl. RM7: Mawney 5B 12
Argyle Gdns. RM14: Upm 1H 33
Argyle Rd. IG1: Ilf 1E 27
Arlington Gdns. IG1: Ilf 6E 19
RM3: Hrld W 5C 14
Armada Way E6 . . . . .5B 34
(Gallions Reach Shop. Pk.)
E6 .6B 34
(Woolwich Mnr. Way)
Armstead Wlk. RM10: Dag 6A 30
Armstrong Cl. RM8: Dag 5F 21
Arncroft Ct. IG11: Bark 3H 35
Arneways Av. RM6: Chad H 1F 21
Arnold Rd. RM9: Dag 6H 29
Arnolds Av. CM13: Hut 1C 6
Arnolds Cl. CM13: Hut 1C 6
Arran Dr. E12 . . . . .6B 18
Arrowsmith Cl. IG7: Chig 2B 10
Arrowsmith Path IG7: Chig 2B 10
Arrowsmith Rd. IG7: Chig 2A 10
Arterial Av. RM13: Rain 4D 38
Artesian Cl. RM11: Horn 4F 23
Arthur Rd. E6 . . . . .2A 34
RM6: Chad H 4E 21
Artillery Cl. IG2: Ilf 4G 19
Artisan Cl. E6 . . . . .6B 34
Arundel Gdns. IG3: Ilf 1C 28
Arundel Rd. RM3: Hrld W 4D 14
Ascension Rd. RM5: Col R 3C 12
Ascot Cl. IG6: Ilf 3A 10
Ascot Gdns. RM12: Horn 3C 32
Ashbeam Cl. CM13: Gt War 3E 17
Ashbourne Av. E18 . . . . .2A 18
Ashbourne Rd. RM3: Rom 1A 14
Ashbrook Rd. RM10: Dag 2B 30
Ashburnham Gdns.
RM14: Upm 6F 25
Ashburton Av. IG3: Ilf 4A 28
Ashbury Gdns. RM6: Chad H 3F 21
Ashby Cl. RM11: Horn 6E 25
Ash Cl. CM15: Pil H 1B 4
RM5: Col R 4B 12
Ashdon Cl. CM13: Hut 2C 6
Ashdown Wlk. RM7: Mawney . . .5B 12
Ashen E6 . . . . .6A 34
Ashford Av. CM14: Bwood 6D 4
Ashford Rd. E6 . . . . .6E 27
E18 .6A 8
Ashgrove Rd. IG3: Ilf 6B 20
Ash La. RM1: Rom 3G 13
RM11: Horn 2D 24
Ashleigh Gdns. RM14: Upm 2H 33
Ashley Av. IG6: Ilf 6F 9
Ashley Rd. E7 . . . . .6A 26
Ashlyn Gro. RM11: Horn 1B 24
Ashmour Gdns. RM1: Rom 6D 12
Ashton Gdns. RM6: Chad H 4G 21
Ashton Ga. RM3: Rom 4B 14
Ashton Rd. RM3: Rom 4B 14
Ashurst Dr. IG2: Ilf 4F 19
IG6: Ilf 3G 19
(Hamilton Av.)
IG6: Ilf 2G 19
(Horns Rd.)
Ashvale Dr. RM14: Upm 5A 40
Ashvale Gdns. RM5: Col R 2D 12
RM14: Upm 5A 40
Ashwood Av. RM13: Rain 4D 38
Askwith Rd. RM13: Rain 3H 37
Aspen Ct. CM13: Bwood 6A 6
Aspen Gro. RM14: Upm 3E 33
Asquith Cl. RM8: Dag 6E 21
Asthall Gdns. IG6: Ilf 2G 19
Aston M. RM6: Chad H 5E 21
Astor Av. RM7: Rom 4C 22
Astra Cl. RM12: Horn 5H 31
Atcost Rd. IG11: Bark 5G 35
Athelstan Cl. RM3: Hrld W 6D 14
Athelstan Rd. RM3: Hrld W 5D 14
Atherton Ho. *RM3: Rom 4C 14*
(off Leyburn Cres.)
Atherton Rd. IG5: Ilf 6C 8
Atholl Rd. IG3: Ilf 5C 20
Atlanta Blvd. RM1: Rom 4E 23
Atlantis Cl. IG11: Bark 3H 35
Aubretia Cl. RM3: Hrld W 5C 14
Auckland Av. RM13: Rain 3B 38
Auckland Rd. IG1: Ilf 6F 19
Audleigh Pl. IG7: Chig 3E 9
Audley Gdns. IG3: Ilf 1B 28
Audrey Rd. IG1: Ilf 2F 27
Auriel Av. RM10: Dag 5D 30
Austin Ct. E6 . . . . .6A 26
Austral Dr. RM11: Horn 5B 24
Aveley Mans. *IG11: Bark 6F 27*
(off Whiting Av.)
Aveley Rd. RM1: Rom 2D 22
RM14: Avel, Upm 5F 33
Avelon Rd. RM5: Col R 3D 12
RM13: Rain 1C 38
Avenue, The CM13: Bwood 3G 17
E11 .3A 18
RM1: Rom 2D 22
RM12: Horn 1A 32
Avenue Cl. RM3: Hrld W 4D 14
Avenue Ind. Est. RM3: Hrld W . . .6B 14
Avenue Rd. CM14: War 1E 17
IG8: Wfd G 3A 8
RM3: Hrld W 4D 14
RM6: Chad H 5D 20
Avery Gdns. IG2: Ilf 3D 18
Avondale Cres. IG4: Ilf 3B 18
Avon Rd. RM14: Upm 4H 25
Axe St. IG11: Bark 1C 34
(not continuous)
Aylett Rd. RM14: Upm 1G 33
Aylmer Rd. RM8: Dag 2G 29
Ayloffe Rd. RM9: Dag 5H 29
Ayloffs Cl. RM11: Horn 2B 24
Ayloffs Wlk. RM11: Horn 3B 24
Aylsham La. RM3: Rom 1A 14
Ayr Grn. RM1: Rom 5E 13
Ayr Way RM1: Rom 5E 13
Azalea Cl. IG1: Ilf 4F 27
Aztec Ho. IG6: Ilf 5G 9

B

Babbacombe Gdns. IG4: Ilf 2C 18
Babington Rd. RM8: Dag 4E 29
RM12: Horn 6H 23
Back La. RM6: Chad H 5F 21
Bacon Link RM5: Col R 3B 12
Bacon Ter. RM8: Dag 4D 28
Baddow Cl. IG8: Wfd G 3A 8
RM10: Dag 1E 37
Baden Powell Cl. RM9: Dag 1C 36
Baden Rd. IG1: Ilf 4F 27
Bader Way RM13: Rain 5G 31
Badger Cl. IG2: Ilf 4G 19
Bagleys Spring RM6: Chad H . . .2G 21
Baillie Cl. RM13: Rain 4D 38
Bainbridge Rd. RM9: Dag 3H 29
Bairny Wood App. IG8: Wfd G 3A 8
Bakers Ct. CM14: Bwood 6E 5
Balfour Rd. IG1: Ilf 1F 27
Balgores Cres. RM2: Rom 1H 23
Balgores La. RM2: Rom 1H 23
Balgores Sq. RM2: Rom 2H 23
Ballards Cl. RM10: Dag 1F 37
Ballards Rd. RM10: Dag 2F 37
Balmoral Gdns. IG3: Ilf 6B 20
Balmoral Rd. CM15: Pil H 2D 4
E7 .3A 26
RM2: Rom 3H 23
RM12: Horn 2B 32
Balmoral Trad. Est.
IG11: Bark 5F 35
Bamber Ho. IG11: Bark 1D 34
Bamford Rd. IG11: Bark 5G 27
Bamford Way RM5: Col R 2B 12
Bampton Rd. RM3: Rom 4C 14
Bancroft Chase RM12: Horn 1F 31
Bank Pl. CM14: Bwood 5E 5
Bankside Pk. IG11: Bark 3G 35
Bankside Rd. IG1: Ilf 4G 27
Banks Way E12 . . . . .3E 27
Bannister Dr. CM13: Hut 2C 6
Banyards RM11: Horn 2C 24
Barberry Cl. RM3: Rom 4A 14
Bardeswell Cl. CM14: Bwood 5E 5
Bardfield Av. RM6: Chad H 1F 21
Barham Cl. RM7: Mawney 6B 12
BARKING 6G 27
Barking Abbey 1C 34
Barking Abbey School Leisure Cen.
. . . . .5C 28
Barking Bus. Pk. IG11: Bark 3G 35
BARKING HOSPITAL 6B 28
Barking Ind. Pk. IG11: Bark 1F 35
Barking Northern Relief Rd.
IG11: Bark 6F 27
BARKING RIVERSIDE 3A 36
Barking Rd. E6 . . . . .1A 34
BARKINGSIDE 1G 19
Barkingside Station (Tube) 1H 19
Barking Station (Rail & Tube)
. . . . .6G 27
Barkwood Cl. RM7: Rom 3C 22
Barleycorn Way RM11: Horn 4D 24
Barleyfields Cl. RM6: Chad H . . .4D 20
Barley La. IG3: Ilf 5C 20
RM6: Chad H 2D 20
Barlow Way RM13: Rain 5H 37
Barnardo Dr. IG6: Ilf 2G 19
Barnardos Village IG6: Ilf 2G 19
Barnes Cl. E12 . . . . .3B 26
Barnes Ct. IG8: Buck H, Wfd G . . .2B 8
Barnes Ho. IG11: Bark 1D 34
Barnes Rd. IG1: Ilf 4G 27
Barnmead Gdns. RM9: Dag 4H 29
Barnmead Rd. RM9: Dag 4H 29
Barnsley Rd. RM3: Rom 4D 14
Barnstaple Path RM3: Rom 2A 14
Barnstaple Rd. RM3: Rom 2A 14
Barnston Way CM13: Hut 1C 6
Baron Gdns. IG6: Ilf 1G 19
Baron Rd. RM8: Dag 6F 21
Barons Ct. IG1: Ilf 1H 27
Barrett Cl. RM3: Rom 4H 13
Barrington Cl. IG5: Ilf 5D 8
Barrington Ct. CM13: Hut 3C 6
Barrington Rd. E12 . . . . .5E 27
Barry Ct. RM5: Col R 2D 12
Bartholomew Dr.
RM3: Hrld W 6B 14
Bartholomew Ho. IG8: Ilf 4F 9
Bartlett Ho's. *RM10: Dag 6B 30*
(off Vicarage Rd.)
Bartlow Gdns. RM5: Col R 5D 12
Barton Av. RM7: Rush G 6B 22
Barton Cl. E6 . . . . .6A 34
Barton Mdws. IG6: Ilf 2F 19
Barton Rd. RM12: Horn 6G 23
Basedale Rd. RM9: Dag 6D 28
Baseing Cl. E6 . . . . .6A 34
Basildon Av. IG5: Ilf 5E 9
Basing Ho. *IG11: Bark 1D 34*
(off St Margarets)
Bassett Ho. RM9: Dag 1H 35
Bassett Rd. E7 . . . . .3B 26
Bastable Av. IG11: Bark 2E 35
Bateman Cl. IG11: Bark 5G 27
Batemans M. CM14: War 1D 16
Bates Bus. Cen. RM3: Hrld W . . .4E 15
Bates Ind. Est. RM3: Hrld W . . .4E 15
Bates Rd. RM3: Hrld W 4E 15
Bath Rd. E7 . . . . .5B 26
RM6: Chad H 4G 21
Bathurst Rd. IG1: Ilf 6F 19
Batten Cl. E6 . . . . .6A 34
Battis, The RM1: Rom 4E 23
Bawdsey Av. IG2: Ilf 2B 20
Baxter Rd. IG1: Ilf 4F 27
Bayleys Mead CM13: Hut 5C 6
Baymans Wood CM15: Shenf 5G 5
Bay Tree Cl. IG6: Ilf 4F 9
Baywood Sq. IG7: Chig 1D 10
Beaconsfield Ter.
RM6: Chad H 4F 21
Beaconsfield Wlk. E6 . . . . .6A 34
BEACONTREE HEATH 6A 22
Beadle's Pde. RM10: Dag 5C 30
Beads Hall La. CM15: Pil H 1D 4
Beal Rd. IG1: Ilf 1E 27
Beam Av. RM10: Dag 1F 37
Beaminster Gdns. IG6: Ilf 6F 9
Beam Vs. RM9: Dag 2G 37
Beamway RM10: Dag 6D 30
Beansland Gro. RM6: Chad H . . .6G 11
Bear Cl. RM7: Rom 4B 22
Beardsley Ter. *RM8: Dag 4D 28*
(off Fitzstephen Rd.)
Bearing Cl. IG7: Chig 1C 10
Bearing Way IG7: Chig 1C 10
Beattyville Gdns. IG6: Ilf 2E 19
Beaufort E6 . . . . .5A 34
Beaufort Cl. RM7: Mawney 2C 22
Beaufort Gdns. IG1: Ilf 6E 19
Beauly Way RM1: Rom 5E 13
Beaumaris Dr. IG8: Wfd G 4B 8
Beaumont Cl. RM2: Rom 6A 14
Beaumont Cres. RM13: Rain 5G 31
Beaumont Gdns. CM13: Hut 2C 6
Beaver Rd. IG6: Ilf 2E 11
Beccles Dr. IG11: Bark 5A 28
Becket Av. E6 . . . . .3A 34

42 A-Z Romford

Becket Cl.—Broadway Theatre, The

Becket Cl. CM13: Gt War 3E **17**
Becketts Ho. IG1: Ilf 2E **27**
BECKTON 5A **34**
BECKTON ALPS 4A **34**
BECKTON PARK 6A **34**
Beckton Retail Pk. E6 5A **34**
Beckton Station (DLR) 5A **34**
Beckton Triangle Retail Pk.
E6 4B **34**
BECONTREE 3F **29**
Becontree Av. RM8: Dag 3D **28**
BECONTREE DAY HOSPITAL 1G 29
Becontree Station (Tube) 5F **29**
Bedale Rd. RM3: Rom 2E **15**
Beddington Rd. IG3: Ilf 5B **20**
Bede Rd. RM6: Chad H 4E **21**
Bedford Gdns. RM12: Horn 1A **32**
Bedford Rd. E6 1A **34**
IG1: Ilf 2F **27**
Bedwell Ct. *RM6: Chad H* 5F **21**
(off Broomfield Rd.)
Beech Av. CM13: Bwood 6H **5**
RM14: Upm 2F **33**
Beech Cl. RM12: Horn 2H **31**
Beech Ct. *IG1: Ilf* 2E **27**
(off Riverdene Rd.)
Beechcroft Rd. E18 6A **8**
Beeches, The CM14: Bwood 6D **4**
E12 6C **26**
Beechfield Gdns.
RM7: Rush G 5C **22**
Beech Gdns. RM10: Dag 6C **30**
Beech Gro. IG6: Ilf 3A **10**
Beech Ho. CM13: Hut 2C **6**
Beech St. RM7: Rom 2C **22**
Beechwood Gdns. IG5: Ilf 3D **18**
RM13: Rain 5D **38**
Beehive Ct. IG1: Ilf 4D **18**
RM3: Hrld W 4D **14**
Beehive La. IG1: Ilf 3D **18**
IG4: Ilf 3D **18**
Belfairs Dr. RM6: Chad H 5E **21**
Belfry Rd. E12 1B **26**
Belgrave Av. RM2: Rom 1A **24**
Belgrave Rd. IG1: Ilf 6D **18**
Bell Av. RM3: Rom 5H **13**
Bell Cnr. RM14: Upm 1G **33**
Belle Vue Rd. RM5: Col R 3C **12**
Bellevue Rd. RM11: Horn 6D **24**
Bell Farm Av. RM10: Dag 2C **30**
Bellflower Path RM3: Rom 4A **14**
Bellhouse La. CM14: Pil H 1A **4**
Bell Ho. Rd. RM7: Rush G 6C **22**
Bellingham Ct. IG11: Bark 3H **35**
Belmont Av. RM14: Upm 1D **32**
Belmont Rd. IG1: Ilf 2G **27**
RM12: Horn 2B **32**
Beltinge Rd. RM3: Hrld W 6D **14**
Belton Rd. E7 6A **26**
Belvedere Av. IG5: Ilf 6F **9**
Belvedere Rd. CM14: Bwood 6B **4**
Bendish Rd. E6 6C **26**
Benedict Ct. RM6: Chad H 4H **21**
Benets Rd. RM11: Horn 6E **25**
Bengal Rd. IG1: Ilf 3F **27**
Bengeo Gdns. RM6: Chad H 4E **21**
Benhurst Av. RM12: Horn 3H **31**
Benjamin Cl. RM11: Horn 4G **23**
Bennett Rd. RM6: Chad H 4G **21**
Bennett's Castle La.
RM8: Dag 1E **29**
Bennions Cl. RM12: Horn 5B **32**
Bennison Dr. RM3: Hrld W 6B **14**
Benrek Cl. IG6: Ilf 5G **9**
Ben Tillet Cl. IG11: Bark 6C **28**
Bentley Dr. IG2: Ilf 4G **19**
Benton Rd. IG1: Ilf 6H **19**
Bentry Cl. RM8: Dag 1G **29**
Bentry Rd. RM8: Dag 1G **29**
Berberis Ct. IG1: Ilf 5F **27**
Beredens La. CM13: Gt War 6B **16**
Beresford Dr. IG8: Wfd G 1A **8**
Beresford Gdns.
RM6: Chad H 3G **21**
Bergholt Av. IG4: Ilf 3C **18**
Berkeley Av. IG5: Ilf 6E **9**
RM5: Col R 4C **12**
Berkeley Cl. RM11: Horn 1F **33**
Berkeley Dr. RM11: Horn 6E **25**
Berkeley Rd. E12 4C **26**
Berkshire Way RM11: Horn 3E **25**
Berman's Cl. CM13: Hut 5B **6**
Bernard Rd. RM7: Rush G 5C **22**
Bernards Cl. IG6: Ilf 4H **9**
Bernice Cl. RM13: Rain 4E **39**
Berry Cl. RM10: Dag 4A **30**
RM12: Horn 4A **32**
Berryman Cl. RM8: Dag 2E **29**
Berther Rd. RM11: Horn 5B **24**
Bertrand Way SE28 6H **35**
Berwick Pond Cl. RM13: Rain 2F **39**
Berwick Pond Rd.
RM13: Rain 2G **39**
RM14: Rain, Upm 6D **32**
Berwick Rd. RM13: Rain 2F **39**
Bessie Lansbury Cl. E6 6A **34**
Betchworth Rd. IG3: Ilf 1A **28**
Bethell Av. IG1: Ilf 5E **19**
Betony Rd. RM3: Rom 3A **14**
Betterton Rd. RM13: Rain 3A **38**
Betula Wlk. RM13: Rain 3F **39**
Beulah Rd. RM12: Horn 2A **32**
Bevan Av. IG11: Bark 6C **28**
Bevan Way RM12: Horn 3D **32**
Beverley Cl. RM11: Horn 5D **24**
Beverley Gdns. RM11: Horn 5D **24**
Beverley Rd. RM9: Dag 3G **29**
Bexley Gdns. RM6: Chad H 3D **20**
Bideford Cl. RM3: Rom 5A **14**
Billet Cl. RM6: Chad H 1F **21**
Billet La. RM11: Horn 6B **24**
Billet Rd. RM6: Chad H 1D **20**
Billing Cl. RM9: Dag 6E **29**
Birch Cl. RM7: Mawney 1B **22**
Birch Ct. RM6: Chad H 4E **21**
Birch Cres. RM11: Horn 2C **24**
Birchdale Gdns. RM6: Chad H 5F **21**
Birchdale Rd. E7 4A **26**
Birches, The CM13: Bwood 6G **5**
E12 3C **26**
Birch Gdns. RM10: Dag 2C **30**
Birch Rd. RM7: Mawney 1B **22**
Birchwood Cl. CM13: Gt War 3E **17**
Birdbrook Cl. CM13: Hut 2B **6**
RM10: Dag 6C **30**
Bird La. RM14: Upm 3H **25**
Birds Farm Av. RM5: Col R 4B **12**
Birkbeck Rd. CM13: Hut 2D **6**
IG2: Ilf 3H **19**
RM7: Rush G 6D **22**
Birkdale Av. RM3: Hrld W 4D **14**
Birkdale Cl. SE28 6B **36**
Bishops Av. RM6: Chad H 4E **21**
Bishop's Hall Rd. CM15: Pil H 2D **4**
Bishop Wlk. CM15: Bwood 5H **5**
Blackborne Rd. RM10: Dag 5A **30**
Blackbush Av. RM6: Chad H 3F **21**
Blacksmiths Cl. RM6: Chad H 4E **21**
Blacksmith's La. RM13: Rain 1B **38**
Blackthorn Rd. IG1: Ilf 4H **27**
Blackthorn Way CM14: War 2F **17**
Blackwater CM14: Bwood 4D **4**
Blackwater Cl. RM13: Rain 5H **37**
Blade Ct. RM7: Rush G 4E **23**
Blake Av. IG11: Bark 1E **35**
Blakeborough Dr.
RM3: Hrld W 6C **14**
Blake Cl. RM13: Rain 1B **38**
Blanchard M. RM3: Hrld W 4D **14**
Blandford Cl. RM7: Mawney 2A **22**
Blaney Cres. E6 3B **34**
Blenheim Av. IG2: Ilf 4E **19**
Blenheim Cl. RM7: Mawney 2C **22**
RM14: Upm 4A **40**
Blenheim Ct. RM12: Horn 4A **32**
Blenheim Rd. CM15: Pil H 2C **4**
Blessing Way IG11: Bark 3A **36**
Blewitts Cotts. *RM13: Rain* 3B **38**
(off New Rd.)
Blithbury Rd. RM9: Dag 5D **28**
Blomville Rd. RM8: Dag 2G **29**
Bloomfield Cres. IG2: Ilf 4F **19**
Blossom Cl. RM9: Dag 1D **36**
Bluebell Av. E12 4B **26**
Bluebell Cl. RM7: Rush G 1E **31**
Bluebell Way IG1: Ilf 5F **27**
Bluebird La. RM10: Dag 6A **30**
Bluegate Pk. CM14: Bwood 6D **4**
Blunden Cl. RM8: Dag 6E **21**
Blythswood Rd. IG3: Ilf 6C **20**
Blyth Wlk. RM14: Upm 2A **40**
Boar Cl. IG7: Chig 2C **10**
Bobs La. RM1: Rom 4G **13**
Boleyn Gdns. CM13: Bwood 6A **6**
RM10: Dag 6C **30**
Boleyn Way IG6: Ilf 3G **9**
Bonham Gdns. RM8: Dag 1F **29**
Bonham Rd. RM8: Dag 1F **29**
Bonington Rd. RM12: Horn 4B **32**
Bonnett M. RM11: Horn 6C **24**
Bonningtons CM13: Bwood 6B **6**
Boomes Ind. Est. RM13: Rain 4B **38**
Booth's Ct. CM13: Hut 2C **6**
Borrowdale Cl. IG4: Ilf 2C **18**
Boscombe Av. RM11: Horn 5B **24**
Bosworth Cres. RM3: Rom 3A **14**
Bosworth Rd. RM10: Dag 2A **30**
Bouchier Wlk. RM13: Rain 5G **31**
Boulevard, The IG8: Ilf 3E **9**
Boulter Gdns. RM13: Rain 5G **31**
Boulton Rd. RM8: Dag 1G **29**
Boundary Cl. IG3: Ilf 3A **28**
Boundary Dr. CM13: Hut 3E **7**
Boundary Rd. IG11: Bark 2C **34**
(Gascoigne Rd.)
IG11: Bark 1D **34**
(King Edwards Rd.)
RM1: Rom 4G **23**
RM14: Upm 2E **33**
Bournebridge Cl. CM13: Hut 3E **7**
Bourne Ct. IG8: Wfd G 1B **18**
Bourne End RM11: Horn 5E **25**
Bowden Dr. RM11: Horn 6C **24**
Bower Cl. RM5: Col R 4D **12**
Bowers RM11: Horn 3B **24**
Bowe's Ho. IG11: Bark 6F **27**
Bowes Rd. RM8: Dag 3E **29**
Bowhay CM13: Hut 5A **6**
Bowland Rd. IG8: Wfd G 3A **8**
Bowls, The IG7: Chig 1A **10**
Bowmont Cl. CM13: Hut 2B **6**
Bowness Way RM12: Horn 4G **31**
Bowyer Cl. E6 5A **34**
Box La. IG11: Bark 2H **35**
Boxmoor Rd. RM5: Col R 2C **12**
Boxoll Rd. RM9: Dag 3H **29**
Boyne Rd. RM10: Dag 2A **30**
Bracken Ct. IG6: Ilf 3B **10**
Brackendale Gdns.
RM14: Upm 3G **33**
Bracken Dr. IG7: Chig 3F **9**
Bracken Ind. Est. IG6: Ilf 4A **10**
Bracken M. RM7: Rom 4B **22**
Brackens Dr. CM14: War 2E **17**
(not continuous)
Brackley Sq. IG8: Wfd G 4B **8**
Braddock Cl. RM5: Col R 3C **12**
Bradfield Dr. IG11: Bark 4C **28**
Bradfield Ho. IG8: Ilf 3E **9**
Bradford Rd. IG1: Ilf 6H **19**
Brading Cres. E11 1A **26**
Bradwell Av. RM10: Dag 1A **30**
Bradwell Cl. RM12: Horn 5H **31**
Bradwell Ct. *CM13: Hut* 2C **6**
(off Bradwell Grn.)
Bradwell Grn. CM13: Hut 2C **6**
Brady Ct. RM8: Dag 6F **21**
Bradymead E6 6A **34**
Braemar Gdns. RM11: Horn 4E **25**
Bragg Cl. RM8: Dag 5D **28**
Braintree Av. IG4: Ilf 2C **18**
Braintree Rd. RM10: Dag 2A **30**
Braithwaite Av. RM7: Rush G 5A **22**
Bramble Ct. IG6: Chig 3B **10**
Brambles, The IG7: Chig 3G **9**
Bramley Cl. IG8: Wfd G 4A **8**
Bramley Cres. IG2: Ilf 4E **19**
Bramshill Cl. IG7: Chig 2A **10**
Bramston Cl. IG6: Ilf 3B **10**
Brancaster Rd. E12 3D **26**
IG2: Ilf 4A **20**
Branch Rd. IG6: Ilf 2D **10**
Brandesbury Sq. IG8: Ilf 4E **9**
Brandreth Rd. E6 6A **34**
Brandville Gdns. IG6: Ilf 2F **19**
Branfill Rd. RM14: Upm 1F **33**
Brantwood Gdns. IG4: Ilf 2C **18**
Breach La. RM9: Dag 3E **37**
Bream Gdns. E6 3A **34**
Breamore Ct. IG3: Ilf 1C **28**
Breamore Rd. IG3: Ilf 1B **28**
Brede Cl. E6 3A **34**
Bredo Ho. IG11: Bark 3H **35**
Brendans Cl. RM11: Horn 6C **24**
Brendon Gdns. IG2: Ilf 3A **20**
Brendon Rd. RM8: Dag 6H **21**
Brentford Pk. Karting Cen. 4E 17
BRENTWOOD 5F **5**
Brentwood By-Pass
CM14: Bwood, S Weald, Pil H
1H **15**
CM15: Bwood, Shenf, Pil H
2E **5**
Brentwood Cathedral 5F 5
Brentwood Cen., The 2E 5
BRENTWOOD COMMUNITY HOSPITAL
4G 5
Brentwood Hard Court Tennis Club
4G 17
Brentwood Lawn Tennis Club 4F 5
Brentwood Mus. 1E 17
Brentwood Pk. Ski &
Snowboarding Cen. 4D 16
Brentwood Pl. CM15: Bwood 4F **5**
Brentwood Rd.
CM13: Heron, Ingve 1H **17**
RM1: Rom 4F **23**
RM2: Rom 4H **23**
Brentwood School Sports Cen. 5F 5
Brentwood Station (Rail) 6E **5**
Brentwood Theatre 4F 5
Bretons Outdoor Recreation Cen.
5F 31
Brett Gdns. RM9: Dag 6G **29**
Brewery, The RM1: Rom 3E **23**
Brewery Wlk. RM1: Rom 3E **23**
Brewood Rd. RM8: Dag 5D **28**
Brian Cl. RM12: Horn 3H **31**
Brian Rd. RM6: Chad H 3E **21**
Briarleas Gdns. RM14: Upm 3A **40**
Briar Rd. RM3: Rom 4A **14**
Briars Wlk. RM3: Hrld W 6D **14**
Brickstock Furze CM15: Shenf 4A **6**
Bridge Av. RM14: Upm 2E **33**
Bridge Cl. CM13: Bwood 6G **5**
RM7: Rush G 4E **23**
Bridgepoint Lofts E7 6A **26**
Bridge Rd. E6 6D **26**
RM13: Rain 4C **38**
Bridgeview Ct. IG6: Ilf 3H **9**
Bridge Wlk. *IG1: Ilf* 1F **27**
(in Exchange, The)
Bridgeway IG11: Bark 6B **28**
Bridgwater Cl. RM3: Rom 2B **14**
Bridgwater Rd. RM3: Rom 2A **14**
Bridgwater Wlk. RM3: Rom 2B **14**
Bridport Av. RM7: Rom 4B **22**
Brierley Cl. RM11: Horn 4A **24**
Brighton Rd. E6 3A **34**
(not continuous)
Brights Av. RM13: Rain 4D **38**
Brindles RM11: Horn 2C **24**
Brindles Cl. CM13: Hut 5C **6**
Brinkworth Rd. IG5: Ilf 1C **18**
Brinsmead Rd. RM3: Hrld W 6E **15**
Brisbane Rd. IG1: Ilf 5F **19**
Briscoe Rd. RM13: Rain 2E **39**
Bristol Ho. *IG11: Bark* 6C **28**
(off Margaret Bondfield Av.)
Bristol Rd. E7 5A **26**
Britannia Rd. CM14: War 2E **17**
IG1: Ilf 2F **27**
Brittain Rd. RM8: Dag 2G **29**
Brixham Gdns. IG3: Ilf 4A **28**
Broadfield Cl. RM1: Rom 3F **23**
Broadfield Way IG9: Buck H 1A **8**
Broadhurst Av. IG3: Ilf 3B **28**
Broadhurst Gdns. IG7: Chig 1G **9**
(not continuous)
Broadhurst Wlk. RM13: Rain 5G **31**
Broadmead Cen. *IG8: Wfd G* 4A **8**
(off Navestock Cres.)
Broadmead Rd. IG8: Wfd G 4A **8**
(not continuous)
Broad Oak IG8: Wfd G 2A **8**
Broadstone Rd. RM12: Horn 1G **31**
Broad St. RM10: Dag 6A **30**
Broad St. Mkt. RM10: Dag 6A **30**
Broad Wlk. Nth., The
CM13: Bwood 6A **6**
(not continuous)
Broad Wlk. Sth., The
CM13: Bwood 6A **6**
Broadway IG11: Bark 1C **34**
RM2: Rom 6G **13**
RM13: Rain 4C **38**
Broadway, The IG8: Wfd G 3A **8**
RM8: Dag 6H **21**
RM12: Horn 3H **31**
Broadway Cl. IG8: Wfd G 3A **8**
Broadway Gdns. IG8: Wfd G 3A **8**
Broadway Mkt. IG6: Ilf 6H **9**
(Forest Rd.)
IG6: Ilf 6G **9**
(Greystone Gdns.)
Broadway Pde. *RM12: Horn* 3H **31**
(off Broadway, The)
Broadway Theatre, The
Barking 1C 34

Brockdish Av.—Chaseside Cl.

Brockdish Av. IG11: Bark 4B 28
Brockenhurst Gdns. IG1: Ilf 4G 27
Brocket Cl. IG7: Chig 1B 10
Brocket Way IG7: Chig 2A 10
Brockham Dr. IG2: Ilf 4F 19
Brockley Cres. RM5: Col R 4C 12
Brockley Gro. CM13: Hut 4A 6
Brocksparkwood CM13: Bwood 6B 6
Brockton Cl. RM1: Rom 2F 23
Bromhall Rd. RM8: Dag 5D 28
Bronte Cl. IG2: Ilf 2E 19
Brook Av. RM10: Dag 6B 30
Brook Cl. RM2: Rom 5F 13
Brook Ct. IG11: Bark 1F 35
Brookdale Av. RM14: Upm 2E 33
Brookdale Cl. RM14: Upm 2F 33
Brooke Trad. Est. RM1: Horn 5F 23
Brookfield Cl. CM13: Hut 2C 6
Brooking Cl. RM8: Dag 2E 29
Brooklands App. RM1: Rom 2D 22
Brooklands Cl. RM7: Rom 2D 22
Brooklands Gdns.
RM11: Horn 4A 24
Brooklands La. RM7: Rom 2D 22
(not continuous)
Brooklands Rd. RM7: Rom 2D 22
Brook Lodge *RM7: Rom 2D 22*
(off Medora Rd.)
Brookmans Cl. RM14: Upm 3A 40
Brook Rd. CM14: Bwood 6B 4
IG2: Ilf 4A 20
RM2: Rom 6F 13
Brooks Av. E6 4A 34
Brooks Ho. CM14: Bwood 4E 5
Brookside IG6: Ilf 3G 9
RM11: Horn 3C 24
BROOK STREET 1B 16
Brook St. CM14: Bwood 2H 15
BROOK STREET INTERCHANGE
1H 15
Brook Way RM13: Rain 5D 38
Broomfield Cl. RM5: Col R 4D 12
Broomfield Rd. RM6: Chad H 5F 21
Broomhill Rd. IG3: Ilf 1C 28
Broomwood Gdns. CM15: Pil H 2C 4
Broseley Gdns. RM3: Rom 1C 14
Broseley Rd. RM3: Rom 1C 14
Browne Cl. CM14: Bwood 4D 4
RM5: Col R 2B 12
Browning Cl. RM5: Col R 4H 11
Browning Rd. E12 4D 26
Brownlea Gdns. IG3: Ilf 1C 28
Broxhill Cen. RM4: Have B 1H 13
Broxhill Rd. RM4: Have B 1E 13
Broxted M. CM13: Hut 2C 6
Bruce Av. RM12: Horn 1A 32
Brunel Cl. RM1: Rom 2E 23
Brunel Rd. IG8: Wfd G 2D 8
Brunswick Av. RM14: Upm 3A 40
Brunswick Ct. RM14: Upm 3B 40
Brunswick Gdns. IG6: Ilf 4G 9
Bryant Av. RM3: Hrld W 5B 14
Bryce Rd. RM8: Dag 3E 29
Buckbean Path RM3: Rom 4A 14
Buckhurst Way IG9: Buck H 1B 8
Buckingham Cl. RM11: Horn 4B 24
Buckingham Rd. E11 3A 18
IG1: Ilf 1H 27
Bucklers Ct. CM14: War 2E 17
Budoch Ct. IG3: Ilf 1C 28
Budoch Dr. IG3: Ilf 1C 28
Buller Rd. IG11: Bark 6A 28
Bull La. RM10: Dag 2B 30
Bulmer Wlk. RM13: Rain 2E 39
Bungalows, The IG6: Ilf 5A 10
Buntingbridge Rd. IG2: Ilf 3H 19
Burchett Way RM6: Chad H 4H 21
Burchwall Cl. RM5: Col R 4C 12
Burden Way E11 1A 26
Burdetts Rd. RM9: Dag 1D 36
Burford Cl. IG6: Ilf 2G 19
RM8: Dag 2E 29
Burge Rd. E7 3B 26
Burges Cl. RM11: Horn 4D 24
Burges Rd. E6 6C 26
Burgess Ct. CM15: Bwood 4F 5
E6 6E 27
Burgess Rd. E6 6E 27
Burland Rd. CM15: Bwood 4F 5
RM5: Col R 3C 12
Burlington Av. RM7: Rom 4B 22
Burlington Gdns.
RM6: Chad H 5G 21
Burnell Wlk. CM13: Gt War 3E 17
Burnels Av. E6 3A 34
Burnett Rd. IG6: Ilf 4F 9
Burnham Cres. E11 2A 18
Burnham Rd. RM7: Rom 1D 22
RM9: Dag 6D 28
Burns Av. RM6: Chad H 5E 21
Burnside Ind. Est. IG6: Ilf 2D 10
Burnside Rd. RM8: Dag 1E 29
Burns Way CM13: Hut 2D 6
Burntwood CM14: Bwood 6E 5
Burntwood Av. RM11: Horn 4B 24
Burnway RM11: Horn 5C 24
Burrow Cl. IG7: Chig 2B 10
Burrow Grn. IG7: Chig 2B 10
Burrow Rd. IG7: Chig 2B 10
Burses Way CM13: Hut 3B 6
Burslem Av. IG6: Ilf 3C 10
Burwood Gdns. RM13: Rain 3B 38
Bury Rd. RM10: Dag 4B 30
Buryside Cl. IG2: Ilf 2B 20
Bush Cl. IG2: Ilf 3H 19
Bush Elms Rd. RM11: Horn 5G 23
Bushgrove Rd. RM8: Dag 3F 29
Bush Rd. IG9: Buck H 1B 8
Bushway RM8: Dag 3F 29
Business Cen., The
RM3: Rom 4B 14
Bute Rd. IG6: Ilf 3F 19
Butler Ct. *RM8: Dag 1A 30*
(off Gosfield Rd.)
Butler Rd. RM8: Dag 3D 28
Buttercup Cl. RM3: Hrld W 5B 14
Butteridges Cl. RM9: Dag 1D 36
Buttfield Cl. RM10: Dag 5B 30
Buttsbury Rd. IG1: Ilf 4G 27
Butts Grn. Rd. RM11: Horn 4B 24
Butts La. CM13: L War 6H 17
Buxton Cl. IG8: Wfd G 3B 8
Buxton Rd. IG2: Ilf 4A 20
Buzzard Creek Ind. Est.
IG11: Bark 5G 35
Byron Av. E12 5C 26
Byron Mans. RM14: Upm 2G 33
Byron Rd. CM13: Hut 3D 6
Byron Way RM3: Rom 5A 14
Bysouth Cl. IG5: Ilf 5F 9
Byway E11 3A 18

C

Cadiz Ct. RM10: Dag 6D 30
Cadiz Rd. RM10: Dag 6C 30
Cadogan Gdns. E18 1A 18
Cadogan Ho. IG8: Ilf 4F 9
Caernarvon Cl. RM11: Horn 6E 25
Caernarvon Dr. IG5: Ilf 5E 9
Cairns Av. IG8: Wfd G 3C 8
Calbourne Av. RM12: Horn 4H 31
Calcott Cl. CM14: Bwood 4D 4
Caledonia Ct. *IG11: Bark 2A 36*
(off Keel Cl.)
Caledonian Cl. IG3: Ilf 6D 20
Caledon Rd. E6 6D 26
Calmore Cl. RM12: Horn 4A 32
Calne Av. IG5: Ilf 5F 9
Calverley Cres. RM10: Dag 1A 30
Calverton Rd. E6 1A 34
Cambeys Rd. RM10: Dag 4B 30
Camborne Av. RM3: Rom 4C 14
Camborne Way RM3: Rom 4C 14
Cambrian Av. IG2: Ilf 3A 20
Cambridge Av. RM2: Rom 1A 24
Cambridge Rd. IG3: Ilf 6A 20
IG11: Bark 6G 27
Camden Rd. E11 4A 18
Camelford Ho. *RM3: Rom 1C 14*
(off Chudleigh Rd.)
Camellia Cl. RM3: Hrld W 5C 14
Cameron Cl. CM14: War 1F 17
Cameron Rd. IG3: Ilf 6A 20
Camomile Rd. RM7: Rush G 1D 30
Campbell Av. IG6: Ilf 2F 19
Campbell Cl. RM1: Rom 3E 13
Campden Cres. RM8: Dag 3D 28
Campion Cl. E6 6A 34
RM7: Rush G 1D 30
Campsey Gdns. RM9: Dag 6D 28
Campsey Rd. RM9: Dag 6D 28
Canalside SE28 6B 36
Canberra Cl. RM10: Dag 1H 37
RM12: Horn 3A 32
Canberra Cres. RM10: Dag 6D 30
Canberra Rd. E6 1A 34
Candover Rd. RM12: Horn 6H 23
Cane Hill RM3: Hrld W 6B 14
Canfield Rd. IG8: Wfd G 4C 8
RM13: Rain 1B 38
Cannington Rd. RM9: Dag 5E 29
Canon Av. RM6: Chad H 3E 21
Canonsleigh Rd. RM9: Dag 6D 28
Canterbury Av. IG1: Ilf 5C 18
RM14: Upm 4B 40
Canterbury Cl. IG7: Chig 1B 10
Canterbury Ct. CM15: Pil H 1B 4
Canterbury Ho. *IG11: Bark 6C 28*
(off Margaret Bondfield Av.)
Canterbury Way
CM13: Gt War 3E 17
Cantley Gdns. IG2: Ilf 4G 19
Cape Cl. IG11: Bark 6F 27
Capel Gdns. IG3: Bark, Ilf 3B 28
Capel Rd. E7 3A 26
E12 3A 26
Capon Cl. CM14: Bwood 4D 4
Capricorn Cen. RM8: Dag 5H 21
Capstan Cl. RM6: Chad H 4D 20
Carbury Cl. RM12: Horn 5A 32
Cardigan Gdns. IG3: Ilf 1C 28
Cardigan Ho. *RM3: Rom 2B 14*
(off Bridgwater Wlk.)
Cardinal Dr. IG6: Ilf 3G 9
Cardinal Way RM13: Rain 2F 39
Carey Rd. RM9: Dag 3G 29
Carfax Rd. RM12: Horn 3F 31
Carisbrooke Cl. RM11: Horn 6E 25
Carisbrooke Rd. CM15: Pil H 2D 4
Carlisle Gdns. IG1: Ilf 4C 18
Carlisle Rd. RM1: Rom 3G 23
Carlton Cl. RM14: Upm 1F 33
Carlton Ct. IG6: Ilf 1H 19
Carlton Dr. IG6: Ilf 1H 19
Carlton Rd. E12 3B 26
RM2: Rom 3F 23
Carlton Ter. St. E7 6A 26
Carlyle Rd. E12 3C 26
Carnation Cl. RM7: Rush G 1E 31
Carnforth Gdns. RM12: Horn 4F 31
Carnoustie Cl. SE28 6B 36
Carpenter Path CM13: Hut 1D 6
Carriage M. IG1: Ilf 1G 27
Carrick Dr. IG6: Ilf 5G 9
Carrow Rd. RM9: Dag 6D 28
Carswell Cl. CM13: Hut 2D 6
IG4: Ilf 2B 18
Carter Cl. RM5: Col R 4A 12
Carter Dr. RM5: Col R 2B 12
Cartwright Rd. RM9: Dag 6H 29
Castellan Av. RM2: Rom 1H 23
Castle Av. RM13: Rain 6E 31
Castle Dr. IG4: Ilf 4C 18
Castle Rd. RM9: Dag 1H 35
Castleton Rd. IG3: Ilf 6C 20
Castleview Gdns. IG1: Ilf 4C 18
Caterham Av. IG5: Ilf 6D 8
Catherine Cl. CM15: Pil H 1C 4
Catherine Ct. IG2: Ilf 3G 19
Catherine Rd. RM2: Rom 3H 23
Caulfield Rd. E6 6C 26
Causton Sq. RM10: Dag 6A 30
Cavalier Cl. RM6: Chad H 2F 21
Cavell Cres. RM3: Hrld W 6C 14
Cavendish Av. RM12: Horn 5H 31
Cavendish Cres. RM12: Horn 5H 31
Cavendish Gdns. IG1: Ilf 6E 19
IG11: Bark 4A 28
RM6: Chad H 3G 21
Cavenham Gdns. IG1: Ilf 2H 27
RM11: Horn 3A 24
Cawdor Ho. CM14: War 1F 17
Caxton Pl. IG1: Ilf 2E 27
Caxton Way RM1: Rom 2E 23
Cecil Av. IG11: Bark 6H 27
RM11: Horn 1C 24
Cecil Rd. IG1: Ilf 3F 27
RM6: Chad H 5F 21
Cedar Av. RM6: Chad H 3G 21
RM14: Upm 3E 33
Cedar Cl. CM13: Hut 3D 6
IG1: Ilf 4H 27
RM7: Rom 2C 22
Cedar Gdns. RM14: Upm 2G 33
Cedar Pk. Gdns. RM6: Chad H 5F 21
Cedar Rd. CM13: Hut 2D 6
RM7: Rom 2C 22
RM12: Horn 2A 32
Cedric Av. RM1: Rom 1E 23
Central Av. E12 2B 26
Central Dr. RM12: Horn 2C 32
Central Gallery *IG1: Ilf 1F 27*
(in Exchange, The)
Central Ho. IG11: Bark 6G 27
Central Pde. IG2: Ilf 4H 19
Central Pk. Av. RM10: Dag 2B 30
Central Pk. Swimming Pool 2C 14
Centre Dr. E7 3A 26
Centre Rd. RM10: Dag 2F 37
Centre Way IG1: Ilf 1G 27
Centro Ct. E6 4A 34
Chadacre Av. IG5: Ilf 1D 18
Chadview Ct. RM6: Chad H 5F 21
Chadville Gdns. RM6: Chad H 3F 21
Chadway RM8: Dag 6E 21
Chadwell Av. RM6: Chad H 5D 20
CHADWELL HEATH 5F 21
Chadwell Heath Ind. Pk.
RM8: Dag 6G 21
Chadwell Heath La.
RM6: Chad H 2D 20
Chadwell Heath Station (Rail)
5F 21
Chadwick Dr. RM3: Hrld W 6B 14
Chadwick Rd. IG1: Ilf 2F 27
Chafford CM14: Bwood 4D 4
Chafford Sports Complex 5E 39
Chafford Wlk. RM13: Rain 2E 39
Chafford Way RM6: Chad H 2E 21
Chalforde Gdns. RM2: Rom 2H 23
Chalford Wlk. IG8: Wfd G 5B 8
Chalgrove Cres. IG5: Ilf 6C 8
Challacombe Cl. CM13: Hut 4B 6
Champion Rd. RM14: Upm 1F 33
Champness Rd. IG11: Bark 5B 28
CHANDLERS CORNER 3E 39
Chandlers Cnr. RM13: Rain 3E 39
Chandlers Way RM1: Rom 3E 23
Channing Cl. RM11: Horn 5D 24
Chantress Cl. RM10: Dag 1G 37
Chantreywood CM13: Bwood 6A 6
Chantry Ho. RM13: Rain 2H 37
Chantry Way RM13: Rain 2H 37
Chapel Av. E12 2B 26
Chapel High *CM14: Bwood 5E 5*
(off High St.)
Chapel High Shop. Cen.
CM14: Bwood 5E 5
Chapel La. IG7: Chig 1B 10
RM6: Chad H 5F 21
Chapel Lodge RM13: Rain 3C 38
Chapel M. IG8: Ilf 3E 9
Chapelmount Rd. IG8: Wfd G 3D 8
Chapel Rd. IG1: Ilf 2E 27
Chaplaincy Gdns.
RM11: Horn 6C 24
Chaplin Rd. RM9: Dag 6G 29
Charlbury Cl. RM3: Rom 3A 14
Charlbury Cres. RM3: Rom 3A 14
Charlbury Gdns. IG3: Ilf 1B 28
Charlecote Rd. RM8: Dag 2G 29
Charlemont Rd. E6 4A 34
Charles Rd. E7 6A 26
RM6: Chad H 4F 21
RM10: Dag 5D 30
CHARLIE BROWN'S RDBT. 6A 8
Charlotte Cl. IG6: Ilf 5G 9
Charlotte Ct. IG2: Ilf 4E 19
RM11: Horn 5B 24
Charlotte Gdns. RM5: Col R 3B 12
Charlotte Rd. RM10: Dag 5B 30
Charlton Cres. IG11: Bark 2F 35
Charnwood Dr. E18 2A 18
Charter Av. IG2: Ilf 6H 19
Charteris Rd. IG8: Wfd G 3A 8
Chart Hills Cl. SE28 6C 36
Chase, The CM14: Bwood 6F 5
CM14: War 1D 16
(Cromwell Rd.)
CM14: War 2F 17
(Woodman Rd.)
E12 3B 26
IG7: Chig 1G 9
RM1: Rom 1E 23
RM6: Chad H 4G 21
RM7: Rush G 2D 30
(not continuous)
RM13: Rain 1D 38
RM14: Upm 6A 40
CHASE CROSS 3E 13
Chase Cross Rd. RM5: Col R 4C 12
Chase Ho. Gdns. RM11: Horn 3D 24
Chase La. IG2: Ilf 3H 19
IG6: Ilf 3H 19
(not continuous)
Chase Nature Reserve, The 2F 31
Chase Rd. CM14: Bwood 6E 5
Chaseside Cl. RM1: Rom 3E 13

Chaseways Vs.—Coxtie Grn. Rd.

Chaseways Vs. RM5: Col R 5H **11**
Chatham Way CM14: Bwood 5E **5**
Chatteris Av. RM3: Rom 3A **14**
Chaucer Rd. RM3: Rom 4H **13**
Cheethams Rd. E12 2C **26**
Chelmer Cres. IG11: Bark 2H **35**
Chelmer Dr. CM13: Hut 2E **7**
Chelmer Rd. RM14: Upm 4H **25**
Chelmsford Av. RM5: Col R 4D **12**
Chelmsford Dr. RM14: Upm 2D **32**
Chelmsford Gdns. IG1: Ilf 5C **18**
Chelmsford Rd. CM15: Shenf 2H **5**
(not continuous)
Chelsea M. RM11: Horn 6H **23**
Chelsworth Cl. RM3: Hrld W 4D **14**
Chelsworth Dr. RM3: Hrld W 5C **14**
Cheltenham Ho. IG8: Ilf 3E **9**
Chepstow Av. RM12: Horn 2C **32**
Chepstow Cres. IG3: Ilf 4A **20**
Chepstow Ho. *RM3: Rom 2E 15*
(off Leamington Rd.)
Chequers La. RM9: Dag 5D **36**
Chequers Pde. RM9: Dag 1D **36**
Cherbury Cl. SE28 6B **36**
Cheriton Av. IG5: Ilf 6D **8**
Cherry Av. CM13: Bwood 6H **5**
Cherry Ct. IG6: Ilf 1F **19**
Cherrydown Wlk.
RM7: Mawney 6B **12**
Cherry Gdns. RM9: Dag 4H **29**
Cherry St. RM7: Rom 3D **22**
Cherry Tree Cl. RM13: Rain 2C **38**
Cherry Tree La. RM13: Rain 3A **38**
Cherry Tree Ri. IG9: Buck H 1A **8**
Cherry Wlk. RM13: Rain 2C **38**
Chertsey Rd. IG1: Ilf 3H **27**
Chesham Cl. RM7: Rom 2D **22**
Chesham Ho. *RM3: Rom 3C 14*
(off Leyburn Cres.)
Cheshire Cl. RM11: Horn 3E **25**
Cheshunt Rd. E7 5A **26**
Chester Av. RM14: Upm 5A **40**
Chesterford Rd. E12 4D **26**
Chester Rd. E7 6B **26**
E11 4A **18**
IG3: Ilf 6B **20**
Chester Ter. IG11: Bark 5H **27**
Chestnut Av. CM14: S Weald 3A **4**
E12 1C **26**
IG9: Buck H 1B **8**
RM12: Horn 1F **31**
Chestnut Cl. RM12: Horn 3A **32**
Chestnut Glen RM12: Horn 1F **31**
Chestnut Gro. CM14: Bwood 5E **5**
IG6: Ilf 3A **10**
Chestnuts CM13: Hut 4B **6**
Cheveley Cl. RM3: Hrld W 5C **14**
Chevington Pl. RM12: Horn 4B **32**
Chevington Way RM12: Horn 3B **32**
Cheviot Rd. RM11: Horn 5G **23**
Cheviot Way IG2: Ilf 2A **20**
Chichester Gdns. IG1: Ilf 5C **18**
Chichester Ho. *CM14: Bwood 5E 5*
(off Sir Francis Way)
CHIGWELL 1F **9**
Chigwell Pk. IG7: Chig 1F **9**
Chigwell Pk. Dr. IG7: Chig 1E **9**
Chigwell Rd. E18 1A **18**
IG8: Wfd G 5A **8**
Chigwell Station (Tube) 1F **9**
Chigwell Vw. RM5: Col R 3A **12**
Childerditch Hall Dr.
CM13: L War 6H **17**
(not continuous)
Childerditch La.
CM13: Bwood, L War 4G **17**
Childers, The IG8: Wfd G 2D **8**
Childs Cl. RM11: Horn 4A **24**
Chiltern Gdns. RM12: Horn 2A **32**
Chiltern Rd. IG2: Ilf 3A **20**
Chindits La. CM14: War 2E **17**
Chippenham Cl. RM3: Rom 2B **14**
Chippenham Gdns. RM3: Rom 2B **14**
Chippenham Rd. RM3: Rom 3B **14**
Chippenham Wlk. RM3: Rom 3B **14**
Chipperfield Cl. RM14: Upm 4A **40**
Chitty's La. RM8: Dag 1F **29**
Choats Mnr. Way RM9: Dag 2C **36**
Choats Rd. IG11: Bark 2A **36**
RM9: Bark, Dag 2A **36**
Christchurch Av. RM13: Rain 2B **38**
Christchurch Rd. IG1: Ilf 6F **19**
Christie Gdns. RM6: Chad H 4D **20**
Christine Ct. RM13: Rain 5C **38**
Christopher Cl. RM12: Horn 3B **32**
Christopher Gdns. RM9: Dag 4F **29**
Chudleigh Cres. IG3: Ilf 3A **28**
Chudleigh Rd. RM3: Rom 1C **14**
Church Av. E12 2B **26**
Church Elm La. RM10: Dag 5A **30**
Church La. CM13: Hut 4E **7**
RM1: Rom 2E **23**
RM10: Dag 6C **30**
RM13: Wenn 6F **39**
Church Path *RM1: Rom 3E 23*
(off Market Pl.)
Church Rd. E12 4C **26**
IG2: Ilf 4A **20**
IG11: Bark 5G **27**
RM3: Hrld W 5E **15**
Church St. RM10: Dag 5B **30**
Church Vw. RM14: Upm 1F **33**
Church Wlk. CM15: Bwood 3D **4**
Churston Av. E13 6A **26**
Cineworld Cinema 2F 27
(off Winston Way)
City Limits Bowling Alley
Collier Row 6H **11**
City of London Crematorium
E12 2C **26**
Civic Way IG6: Ilf 2G **19**
Claire Cl.
CM13: Bwood 1H **17** & 6A **6**
Clairvale RM11: Horn 5C **24**
Clandon Rd. IG3: Ilf 1A **28**
Clap La. RM10: Dag, Rush G 1B **30**
Claps Ga. La. E6 4A **34**
Clare Gdns. IG11: Bark 5B **28**
Claremont Gdns. IG3: Ilf 1A **28**
RM14: Upm 6H **25**
Claremont Gro. IG8: Wfd G 3A **8**
Claremont Rd. E7 4A **26**
RM11: Horn 4G **23**
Clarence Av. IG2: Ilf 4E **19**
RM14: Upm 1E **33**
Clarence Ga. IG8: Ilf, Wfd G 3E **9**
Clarence Rd. CM15: Pil H 2D **4**
E12 3A **26**
Clarendon Gdns. IG1: Ilf 5D **18**
Claridge Rd. RM8: Dag 6F **21**
Clarissa Rd. RM6: Chad H 5F **21**
Clarke Mans. *IG11: Bark 6B 28*
(off Upney La.)
Clarksons, The IG11: Bark 2C **34**
Clarks Rd. IG1: Ilf 1H **27**
Claughton Way CM13: Hut 2D **6**
Clavering Rd. E12 6B **18**
Clavering Way CM13: Hut 2C **6**
Claybury B'way. IG5: Ilf 1C **18**
Claybury Hill IG8: Wfd G 4D **8**
Claybury Rd. IG8: Wfd G 4C **8**
Claygate Cl. RM12: Horn 3G **31**
CLAYHALL 1C **18**
Clayhall Av. IG5: Ilf 1C **18**
Clayside IG7: Chig 2G **9**
Clayton Av. RM14: Upm 4F **33**
Clayton Cl. E6 6A **34**
Clayton Rd. RM7: Rush G 6C **22**
Clematis Cl. RM3: Rom 4A **14**
Clemence Rd. RM10: Dag 1G **37**
Clementhorpe Rd.
RM9: Dag 5E **29**
Clements Ct. IG1: Ilf 2F **27**
Clements La. IG1: Ilf 2F **27**
Clements Rd. E6 6C **26**
IG1: Ilf 2F **27**
Clement Way RM14: Upm 2D **32**
Cleveland Rd. IG1: Ilf 2F **27**
Clevelands, The IG11: Bark 5G **27**
Cleves Av. CM14: Bwood 4D **4**
Cleves Wlk. IG6: Ilf 4G **9**
Clifford Av. IG5: Ilf 5F **9**
Clifton Rd. E7 5B **26**
IG2: Ilf 4H **19**
RM11: Horn 4G **23**
Clifton Way CM13: Hut 4D **6**
Clinton Cres. IG6: Ilf 3A **10**
Clitheroe Rd. RM5: Col R 2C **12**
Cliveden Cl. CM15: Shenf 3H **5**
Clive Rd. CM13: Gt War 4E **17**
RM2: Rom 3H **23**
Clockhouse Av. IG11: Bark 1C **34**
Clockhouse La. RM4: Have B 1B **12**
RM5: Col R 4B **12**
Cloister Cl. RM13: Rain 4D **38**
Close, The CM14: Bwood 6F **5**
IG2: Ilf 4A **20**
RM6: Chad H 4G **21**
Cloudberry Rd. RM3: Rom 3B **14**
Clovelly Ct. RM11: Horn 1E **33**
Clovelly Gdns. RM7: Mawney 5B **12**
Cluff Ct. CM14: War 1E **17**
Clunas Gdns. RM2: Rom 1B **24**
Clune Ct. CM15: Shenf 3A **6**
Clyde Cres. RM14: Upm 2A **40**
Clydesdale Rd. RM11: Horn 5F **23**
Clyde Way RM1: Rom 4E **13**
Clynes Ho. *RM10: Dag 2A 30*
(off Uvedale Rd.)
Cobbetts Av. IG4: Ilf 3B **18**
Cobbles, The CM15: Bwood 5G **5**
RM14: Upm 3B **40**
Cobdens IG7: Chig 3H **9**
Cobham Ho. IG11: Bark 1C **34**
(not continuous)
Cobham Rd. IG3: Ilf 1A **28**
Cobill Cl. RM11: Horn 2A **24**
Coburg Gdns. IG5: Ilf 6B **8**
Cockabourne Ct. *RM3: Hrld W 6E 15*
(off Archibald Rd.)
Codham Hall La.
CM13: Gt War 1D **40**
(not continuous)
Colchester Av. E12 3D **26**
Colchester Rd.
CM14: Bwood, Hrld W 5B **14**
RM3: Hrld W, Rom 5B **14**
Coldharbour La. RM13: Rain 6A **38**
Colebrooke Dr. E11 5A **18**
Cole Ct. RM3: Rom 2C **14**
Coleford Ho. *RM3: Rom 3C 14*
(off Kingsbridge Rd.)
Coleman Rd. RM9: Dag 5G **29**
Colenso Rd. IG2: Ilf 6A **20**
Coleridge Av. E12 5C **26**
Coleridge Rd. RM3: Rom 4H **13**
Coleridge Wlk. CM13: Hut 3C **6**
Colet Rd. CM13: Hut 1C **6**
Colinton Rd. IG3: Ilf 1D **28**
College Ct. *RM2: Rom 3H 23*
(off Scholars Way)
College Gdns. IG4: Ilf 3C **18**
Collier Cl. E6 6B **34**
COLLIER ROW 4B **12**
Collier Row La. RM5: Col R 4B **12**
Collier Row Rd. RM5: Col R 5H **11**
Collingwood Cl. RM13: Rain 2B **38**
Collins Way CM13: Hut 1F **7**
Collinwood Gdns. IG5: Ilf 3D **18**
Colne Dr. RM3: Rom 3D **14**
Colne Ho. IG11: Bark 6F **27**
Colne Valley RM14: Upm 2A **40**
Colombo Rd. IG1: Ilf 6G **19**
Colston Rd. E7 5B **26**
Coltishall Rd. RM12: Horn 5A **32**
Coltsfoot Path RM3: Rom 4A **14**
(not continuous)
Columbine Way RM3: Hrld W 5C **14**
Colvin Gdns. E11 2A **18**
IG6: Ilf 5G **9**
Colvin Rd. E6 6C **26**
Comet Cl. E12 3B **26**
Como St. RM7: Rom 3D **22**
Compton Av. CM13: Hut 4C **6**
RM2: Rom 1A **24**
Comyns Rd. RM9: Dag 6A **30**
Concorde Ho. *RM12: Horn 5H 31*
(off Astra Cl.)
Condor Wlk. RM12: Horn 6H **31**
Conifer Av. RM5: Col R 2B **12**
Conifer Dr. CM14: War 2F **17**
Coniston Av. IG11: Bark 6A **28**
RM14: Upm 3G **33**
Coniston Cl. IG11: Bark 6A **28**
Coniston Gdns. IG4: Ilf 2C **18**
Coniston Way RM12: Horn 4G **31**
Connaught La. IG1: Ilf 1G **27**
Connaught Rd. IG1: Ilf 1H **27**
RM12: Horn 2B **32**
Connor Cl. IG6: Ilf 5G **9**
Connor Rd. RM9: Dag 3H **29**
Conqueror Ct. RM3: Rom 4B **14**
Consort Cl. CM14: War 2E **17**
Constable M. RM8: Dag 3D **28**
Consul Av. RM9: Dag, Rain 3G **37**
RM13: Rain 3G **37**
Conway Cl. RM13: Rain 6G **31**
Conway Cres. RM6: Chad H 4E **21**
Cooke St. IG11: Bark 1C **34**
Cook Rd. RM9: Dag 1C **36**
Cook's Cl. RM5: Col R 5C **12**
Coolgardie Av. IG7: Chig 1E **9**
Coombe Ri. CM15: Shenf 4H **5**
Coombe Rd. RM3: Hrld W 1D **24**
Coombes Rd. RM9: Dag 1D **36**
Coombewood Dr.
RM6: Chad H 4H **21**
Coopersale Cl. IG8: Wfd G 4A **8**
Coopers Cl. RM10: Dag 5B **30**
Coote Gdns. RM8: Dag 2H **29**
Coote Rd. RM8: Dag 2H **29**
Copeman Rd. CM13: Hut 3D **6**
Copford Cl. IG8: Wfd G 3C **8**
Coppen Rd. RM8: Dag 5H **21**
Copper Beech Cl. IG5: Ilf 5E **9**
Copperfield IG7: Chig 2H **9**
Copperfield Gdns.
CM14: Bwood 4D **4**
Copperfield Rd. SE28 6A **36**
Copperfields Way
RM3: Hrld W 5B **14**
Coppice Path IG7: Chig 1D **10**
Coptfold Rd. CM14: Bwood 5E **5**
Copthorne Av. IG6: Ilf 3F **9**
Copthorne Gdns. RM11: Horn 3E **25**
Coral Cl. RM6: Chad H 2E **21**
Coram Grn. CM13: Hut 2D **6**
Corbets Av. RM14: Upm 4F **33**
CORBETS TEY 4G **33**
Corbets Tey Rd. RM14: Upm 3F **33**
Corbett Rd. E11 4A **18**
Corbridge M. RM1: Rom 3F **23**
Corcorans CM15: Pil H 2D **4**
Cories Cl. RM8: Dag 1F **29**
Corkers Path IG1: Ilf 1G **27**
Cormorant Wlk. RM12: Horn 5H **31**
Cornell Way RM5: Col R 2A **12**
Cornflower Way RM3: Hrld W 5C **14**
Cornshaw Rd. RM8: Dag 6F **21**
Cornsland CM14: Bwood 6F **5**
Cornsland Cl. RM14: Upm 1G **25**
Cornsland Ct. CM14: Bwood 6E **5**
Cornwall Cl. IG11: Bark 5B **28**
RM11: Horn 2E **25**
Cornwallis Rd. RM9: Dag 3F **29**
Cornwall Rd. CM15: Pil H 1D **4**
Cornwell Cres. E7 3A **26**
Cornworthy Rd. RM8: Dag 4E **29**
Coronation Cl. IG6: Ilf 2G **19**
Coronation Dr. RM12: Horn 4H **31**
Cory Dr. CM13: Hut 3B **6**
Costead Mnr. Rd.
CM14: Bwood 4D **4**
Cotesmore Gdns. RM8: Dag 3E **29**
Cotleigh Rd. RM7: Rom 4D **22**
Cotman M. *RM8: Dag 4E 29*
(off Highgrove Rd.)
Cotswold Gdns. CM13: Hut 3E **7**
IG2: Ilf 5H **19**
Cotswold Rd. RM3: Hrld W 6D **14**
Cottage M. RM11: Horn 2A **24**
Cottesmore Av. IG5: Ilf 6E **9**
Cotton Cl. RM9: Dag 6E **29**
Cottons App. RM7: Rom 3D **22**
Cottons Ct. RM7: Rom 3D **22**
Couchmore Av. IG5: Ilf 6D **8**
Coulson Cl. RM8: Dag 6E **21**
County Gdns. IG11: Bark 2E **35**
County Rd. E6 5B **34**
Courage Cl. RM11: Horn 4A **24**
Courage Ct. CM13: Hut 2C **6**
Courage Wlk. CM13: Hut 2D **6**
Courier Rd. RM9: Dag 4G **37**
RM13: Dag 4G **37**
Court Av. RM3: Hrld W 4E **15**
Courtenay Gdns. RM14: Upm 6G **25**
Court Gdns. RM3: Hrld W 3E **15**
Courtland Av. IG1: Ilf 1D **26**
Courtland Cl. IG8: Wfd G 5A **8**
Courtland Gro. SE28 6B **36**
Court Way IG6: Ilf 1G **19**
IG8: Wfd G 2A **8**
RM3: Hrld W 6C **14**
Courtyard, The CM15: Bwood 3D **4**
Covelees Wall E6 6A **34**
Covenbrook CM13: Bwood 6B **6**
Coventry Rd. IG1: Ilf 1F **27**
Coverdales, The IG11: Bark 2D **34**
Coverley Cl. CM13: Gt War 3E **17**
Covert Rd. IG6: Ilf 2B **10**
Coverts, The CM13: Hut 4A **6**
Cowbridge La. IG11: Bark 6F **27**
Cowdray Way RM12: Horn 3G **31**
Cow Leaze E6 6A **34**
Cowley Rd. IG1: Ilf 5D **18**
RM3: Rom 4H **13**
Cowper Av. E6 6C **26**
Cowper Rd. RM13: Rain 4C **38**
Coxtie Grn. Rd.
CM14: S Weald, Pil H 1A **4**

G

Great Oaks—Helmore Rd.

Great Oaks CM13: Hut 2B 6
IG7: Chig 1G 9
Gt. Ropers La. CM14: Gt War 3C 16
GREAT WARLEY 5C 16
Gt. Warley St. CM13: Gt War 5C 16
Greaves Cl. IG11: Bark 6H 27
Grebe Cl. IG11: Bark 4G 35
Greding Wlk. CM13: Hut 5B 6
Green, The RM13: Wenn 6G 39
Greenacres Cl. RM13: Rain 3G 39
Green Banks RM14: Upm 5A 40
Greenfield Gdns. RM9: Dag 1B 36
Greenfield Rd. RM9: Dag 6E 29
Greenfields Cl. CM13: Gt War 3E 17
Greengate Pde. IG2: Ilf 4H 19
Green Glades RM11: Horn 4D 24
Greenhaven Dr. SE28 6H 35
Greenhill Gro. E12 3C 26
Green La. CM14: Bwood 4C 4
CM14: Gt War 4C 16
CM15: Pil H 1E 5
IG1: Ilf 1H 27
IG3: Ilf 6D 20
RM8: Dag 6D 20
Greenleafe Dr. IG6: Ilf 1F 19
Greenock Way RM1: Rom 4E 13
Greenshaw CM14: Bwood 4D 4
Green Side RM8: Dag 6E 21
Greenslade Rd. IG11: Bark 6H 27
Greensleeves Dr.
CM14: Gt War 2D 16
Greenstead Av. IG8: Wfd G 4A 8
Greenstead Cl. CM13: Hut 3E 7
IG8: Wfd G 3A 8
Greenstead Gdns. IG8: Wfd G 3A 8
Green St. E7 5A 26
E13 5A 26
Green Wlk. IG8: Wfd G 3C 8
Green Way IG8: Wfd G 2A 8
Greenway CM13: Hut 3A 6
RM3: Hrld W 3F 15
RM8: Dag 1E 29
Greenway Ct. IG1: Ilf 6E 19
Greenways Ct. RM11: Horn 4B 24
Greenwood Av. RM10: Dag 3B 30
Greenwood Gdns. IG6: Ilf 4G 9
Greenwood Mans. *IG11: Bark* 6C 28
(off Lansbury Av.)
Greenwood Rd. IG7: Chig 1D 10
Gregory Rd. RM6: Chad H 2F 21
Grenfell Av. RM12: Horn 6F 23
Grenfell Gdns. IG3: Ilf 3B 20
Grenville Gdns. IG8: Wfd G 5A 8
Gresham Cl. CM14: Bwood 6E 5
Gresham Ct. CM14: Bwood 6E 5
Gresham Dr. RM6: Chad H 3D 20
Gresham Rd. CM14: Bwood 6E 5
E6 2A 34
Greville Lodge E13 6A 26
Greyfriars CM13: Hut 3B 6
Greystone Gdns. IG6: Ilf 6G 9
Grey Towers Av. RM11: Horn 5B 24
Grey Towers Gdns.
RM11: Horn 5A 24
Gridiron Pl. RM14: Upm 2F 33
Griffin Av. RM14: Upm 2A 40
Griffith Cl. RM8: Dag 5E 21
Griggs App. IG1: Ilf 1G 27
Griggs Gdns. RM12: Horn 4A 32
Grimshaw Way RM1: Rom 3F 23
Grimstone Cl. RM5: Col R 3B 12
Grosvenor Dr. RM11: Horn 6A 24
Grosvenor Gdns. RM14: Upm 6H 25
Grosvenor Rd. E7 5A 26
E11 3A 18
IG1: Ilf 2G 27
RM7: Rush G 5D 22
RM8: Dag 6H 21
Grove, The CM14: Bwood 1B 16
RM14: Upm 3F 33
Grove Ct. RM14: Upm 3E 33
Grove Farm Retail Pk.
RM6: Chad H 5E 21
Grove Gdns. RM10: Dag 2C 30
Grove Ho. CM14: War 1D 16
Grove La. IG7: Chig 1B 10
Grove Pk. E11 3A 18
Grove Pk. Rd. RM13: Rain 1C 38
Grove Pl. IG11: Bark 6G 27
Grove Rd. RM6: Chad H 5D 20
Groveway RM8: Dag 3F 29
Grovewood Pl. IG8: Wfd G 3D 8
Guardian Bus. Cen.
RM3: Rom 4B 14
Guardian Cl. RM11: Horn 1H 31
Guardsman Cl. CM14: War 2F 17
Gubbins La. RM3: Hrld W 4D 14
Guildford Gdns. RM3: Rom 3C 14
Guildford Rd. IG3: Ilf 1A 28
RM3: Rom 3C 14
Gull Wlk. RM12: Horn 6H 31
Gurney Cl. IG11: Bark 5F 27
Guysfield Cl. RM13: Rain 1C 38
Guysfield Dr. RM13: Rain 1C 38
Gwynne Pk. Av. IG8: Wfd G 3D 8
Gyllyngdune Gdns. IG3: Ilf 1B 28

H

HACTON 4D 32
Hacton Dr. RM12: Horn 3B 32
Hacton La. RM12: Horn, Upm 1D 32
RM14: Upm 4D 32
Hacton Pde. RM12: Horn 2D 32
Hadleigh Ct. CM14: Bwood 6C 4
Haigville Gdns. IG6: Ilf 2F 19
Hailsham Cl. RM3: Rom 2A 14
Hailsham Gdns. RM3: Rom 2A 14
Hailsham Rd. RM3: Rom 2A 14
HAINAULT 2B 10
Hainault Bus. Pk. IG6: Ilf 2E 11
Hainault Forest Country Pk. 1F 11
Hainault Forest Country Pk. Vis. Cen. 1F 11
Hainault Gore RM6: Chad H 3G 21
Hainault Gro. IG7: Chig 1G 9
Hainault Ind. Est. IG6: Ilf 2E 11
Hainault Rd. IG7: Chig 1F 9
RM5: Col R, Rom 6C 12
RM6: Chad H 4D 10
(Forest Rd.)
RM6: Chad H 4H 21
(High Rd.)
Hainault Station (Tube) 4A 10
Hainault St. IG1: Ilf 1G 27
Halbutt Gdns. RM9: Dag 2H 29
Halbutt St. RM9: Dag 3H 29
Halcyon Way RM11: Horn 6D 24
Haldon Cl. IG7: Chig 2A 10
Hale End RM3: Rom 3H 13
Hale Ho. *RM11: Horn* 4G 23
(off Benjamin Cl.)
Halesworth Cl. RM3: Rom 4C 14
Halesworth Rd. RM3: Rom 3C 14
Halidon Ri. RM3: Hrld W 3F 15
Halifax Ho. *RM3: Rom* 2C 14
(off Lindfield Rd.)
Halley Rd. E7 5A 26
E12 5A 26
Hall Grn. La. CM13: Hut 3C 6
Hall La. RM14: Upm 6G 15
Hall Pk. Rd. RM14: Upm 4G 33
Hall Rd. E6 6D 26
RM2: Rom 1H 23
RM6: Chad H 4E 21
Hall Ter. RM3: Hrld W 4E 15
Hallwood Cres. CM15: Shenf 3G 5
Hallywell Cres. E6 5A 34
Halsham Cres. IG11: Bark 4B 28
Halstead Ho. *RM3: Rom* 3B 14
(off Dartfields)
Halstead Way CM13: Hut 2C 6
Hamden Cres. RM10: Dag 2B 30
Hame Way E6 4A 34
Hamilton Av. IG6: Ilf 2F 19
RM1: Rom 6D 12
Hamilton Cres. CM14: War 1E 17
Hamilton Dr. RM3: Hrld W 6C 14
Hamilton Rd. IG1: Ilf 3F 27
RM2: Rom 3H 23
Hamlet Cl. RM5: Col R 4A 12
Hamlet Rd. RM5: Col R 4A 12
Hammond Ct. RM12: Horn 6F 23
Hammonds Cl. RM8: Dag 2E 29
Hammonds La. CM13: Gt War 3D 16
Hampden Cres. CM14: War 1E 17
Hampden Rd. RM5: Col R 4B 12
Hampshire Rd. RM11: Horn 2E 25
Hampstead Av. IG8: Wfd G 4E 9
Hampstead Gdns.
RM6: Chad H 3D 20
Hampton Rd. E7 4A 26
IG1: Ilf 3G 27
Handforth Rd. IG1: Ilf 2F 27
Handtrough Way IG11: Bark 2B 34
Hanging Hill La.
CM13: Bwood, Hut 6B 6
Hannards Way IG6: Ilf 2D 10
Hanover Gdns. IG6: Ilf 4G 9
Hanover Pl. CM14: Gt War 2D 16
Harbourer Cl. IG6: Ilf 2D 10
Harbourer Rd. IG6: Ilf 2D 10
Harcourt Av. E12 3D 26
Harcourt M. RM2: Rom 3F 23
Hardie Rd. RM10: Dag 2C 30
Hardley Cres. RM11: Horn 2B 24
Hardwicke St. IG11: Bark 1C 34
Harebell Dr. E6 5A 34
Harebell Way RM3: Rom 4B 14
Harehall La. RM2: Rom 2H 23
Haresfield Rd. RM10: Dag 5A 30
Harewood Dr. IG5: Ilf 6D 8
Harewood Rd. CM15: Pil H 2D 4
Harkness Cl. RM3: Rom 2D 14
Harlesden Cl. RM3: Rom 3D 14
Harlesden Rd. RM3: Rom 3D 14
Harlesden Wlk. RM3: Rom 4D 14
Harlow Gdns. RM5: Col R 3C 12
Harlow Mans. *IG11: Bark* 6F 27
(off Whiting Av.)
Harlow Rd. RM13: Rain 1B 38
Harold Ct. RM3: Hrld W 4F 15
Harold Ct. Rd. RM3: Hrld W 3F 15
HAROLD HILL 3D 14
Harold Hill Ind. Est.
RM3: Rom 4B 14
HAROLD PARK 3F 15
Harold Vw. RM3: Hrld W 6D 14
HAROLD WOOD 5D 14
Harold Wood Hall *RM3: Rom* 5B 14
(off Widecombe Cl.)
HAROLD WOOD HOSPITAL 5C 14
Harold Wood Station (Rail) 5D 14
Harpenden Rd. E12 1A 26
Harpour Rd. IG11: Bark 5G 27
Harrier Av. E11 4A 18
Harrier Cl. RM12: Horn 5H 31
Harrier Way E6 5A 34
Harris Cl. RM3: Rom 4C 14
Harrison Cl. CM13: Hut 1D 6
Harrison Rd. RM10: Dag 5B 30
Harris Rd. RM9: Dag 4H 29
Harrold Rd. RM8: Dag 4D 28
Harrow Cl. RM11: Horn 6H 23
Harrow Cres. RM3: Rom 4H 13
Harrow Dr. RM11: Horn 4H 23
Harrow Rd. IG1: Ilf 3G 27
IG11: Bark 1E 35
Hart Ct. E6 6E 27
Hart Cres. IG7: Chig 2B 10
Hartland Rd. RM12: Horn 1G 31
Hartshorn Gdns. E6 4A 34
Harts La. IG11: Bark 5F 27
Hart St. CM14: Bwood 5E 5
HARTSWOOD BUPA HOSPITAL 3D 16
Hartswood Cl. CM14: War 1G 17
Hartswood Rd. CM13: Gt War 1G 17
CM14: War 1G 17
Harvard Wlk. RM12: Horn 3G 31
Harvey Ho. RM6: Chad H 2F 21
Harvey Rd. IG1: Ilf 4F 27
Harveys La. RM7: Rush G 1D 30
Harwood Av. RM11: Horn 1C 24
Harwood Hall La. RM14: Upm 5F 33
Haskard Rd. RM9: Dag 3F 29
Haslemere Rd. IG3: Ilf 1B 28
Haslingden Ho. *RM3: Rom* 2C 14
(off Dagnam Pk. Dr.)
Hastings Av. IG6: Ilf 2G 19
Hastings Rd. RM2: Rom 3H 23
Hatch Gro. RM6: Chad H 2G 21
Hatch Rd. CM15: Pil H 1C 4
Hatch Side IG7: Chig 2E 9
Hatfield Cl. CM13: Hut 3D 6
IG6: Ilf 1F 19
RM12: Horn 4B 32
Hatfield Rd. RM9: Dag 5G 29
Hathaway Cl. IG6: Ilf 3F 9
Hathaway Cres. E12 5D 26
Hathaway Gdns. RM6: Chad H 3F 21
Hatherleigh Way RM3: Rom 5B 14
Hatley Av. IG6: Ilf 2G 19
Havana Cl. RM1: Rom 3E 23
RM3: Rom 2C 14
(off Gooshays Dr.)
Havant Ho. *RM3: Rom* 4C 14
(off Kingsbridge Cir.)
Havelock St. IG1: Ilf 1F 27
Havenwood Cl. CM13: Gt War 3E 17
HAVERING-ATTE-BOWER 1D 12
Havering Country Pk. 1C 12
Havering Dr. RM1: Rom 2E 23
Havering Gdns. RM6: Chad H 3E 21
HAVERING PARK 2B 12
Havering Rd.
RM1: Have B, Rom 2D 12
HAVERING'S GROVE 3H 7
Havering Way IG11: Bark 3H 35
Hawkhurst Gdns. RM5: Col R 3D 12
Hawkinge Way RM12: Horn 5A 32
Hawkridge Cl. RM6: Chad H 4E 21
Hawksmoor Grn. CM13: Hut 1D 6
(not continuous)
Hawkwell Ho. RM8: Dag 6A 22
Hawthorn Av. CM13: Bwood 6H 5
RM13: Rain 4D 38
Hawthorn Rd. IG9: Buck H 1B 8
Hayburn Way RM12: Horn 6F 23
Hayden Way RM5: Col R 6C 12
Haydock Cl. RM12: Horn 3D 32
Haydon Cl. RM3: Rom 4H 13
Haydon Rd. RM8: Dag 1E 29
Hayes Dr. RM13: Rain 6H 31
Hay Grn. RM11: Horn 4E 25
Haynes Rd. RM11: Horn 2B 24
Haysoms Cl. RM1: Rom 2E 23
Hayter Ct. E11 1A 26
Haywards Cl. CM13: Hut 2E 7
RM6: Chad H 3D 20
Hazelbrouck Gdns. IG6: Ilf 4H 9
Hazel Cl. RM12: Horn 2H 31
Hazel Cres. RM5: Col R 5B 12
Hazeldene Rd. IG3: Ilf 1D 28
Hazeleigh CM13: Bwood 6B 6
Hazeleigh Gdns. IG8: Wfd G 2C 8
Hazel Gro. RM6: Chad H 1G 21
Hazel La. IG6: Ilf 3F 9
Hazelmere Gdns.
RM11: Horn 3A 24
Hazel Ri. RM11: Horn 4A 24
Hazelwood Gdns. CM15: Pil H 2C 4
Hazelwood Pk. Cl. IG7: Chig 2A 10
Hazle Ceramics Workshop 1D 40
Headingley Cl. IG6: Ilf 3B 10
Headley App. IG2: Ilf 3F 19
Headley Chase CM14: War 1E 17
Headley Dr. IG2: Ilf 4F 19
Hearn Rd. RM1: Rom 4F 23
Heath Cl. RM2: Rom 1G 23
Heathcote Av. IG5: Ilf 6D 8
Heathcote Ct. IG5: Ilf 5D 8
(Glade Ct.)
IG5: Ilf 6D 8
(Heathcote Av.)
Heath Dr. RM2: Rom 5G 13
Heather Av. RM1: Rom 6D 12
Heather Cl. CM15: Pil H 1D 4
E6 6A 34
RM1: Rom 5D 12
Heather Dr. RM1: Rom 6D 12
Heather Gdns. RM1: Rom 6D 12
Heather Glen RM1: Rom 6D 12
Heatherley Dr. IG5: Ilf 1C 18
Heather Way RM1: Rom 6D 12
Heatherwood Cl. E12 1A 26
Heathfield Pk. Dr.
RM6: Chad H 3D 20
HEATH PARK 4G 23
Heath Pk. Ct. RM2: Rom 3G 23
Heath Pk. Rd. RM1: Rom 3G 23
RM2: Rom 3G 23
Heath Rd. RM6: Chad H 5F 21
Heathside Cl. IG2: Ilf 3H 19
HEATHWAY 1E 37
Heath Way IG8: Wfd G 2A 8
Heathway RM9: Dag 2H 29
RM10: Dag 2H 29
Heathway Ind. Est.
RM10: Dag 3B 30
Heaton Av. RM3: Rom 4H 13
Heaton Cl. RM3: Rom 4A 14
Heaton Grange Rd.
RM2: Rom 6F 13
Heaton Way RM3: Rom 4A 14
Hedgeley IG4: Ilf 2D 18
Hedgemans Rd. RM9: Dag 6F 29
Hedgemans Way RM9: Dag 5G 29
Hedgerows CM13: Hut 2E 7
Hedgewood Gdns. IG5: Ilf 3E 19
Hedingham Rd. RM8: Dag 4D 28
RM11: Horn 6E 25
Hedley Ct. RM1: Rom 3E 23
Heenan Cl. IG11: Bark 5G 27
Heideck Gdns. CM13: Hut 5B 6
Heigham Rd. E6 6C 26
Helen Rd. RM11: Horn 1B 24
Helford Way RM14: Upm 4H 25
Helmore Rd. IG11: Bark 6B 28

Lichfield Ter.—Marwell Cl.

Lichfield Ter. RM14: Upm 5A 40
Lilac Cl. CM15: Pil H 1D 4
Lilac Gdns. RM7: Rush G 6E 23
Lilian Cres. CM13: Hut 5C 6
Lilian Gdns. IG8: Wfd G 5A 8
Lillechurch Rd. RM8: Dag 5D 28
Lilley Cl. CM14: Bwood 1B 16
Lilliput Rd. RM7: Rush G 5D 22
Limbourne Av. RM8: Dag 5H 21
Lime Av. CM13: Bwood 6H 5
RM14: Upm 3E 33
Lime Cl. RM7: Rom 2C 22
Lime Gro. IG6: Ilf 3B 10
Limerick Gdns. RM14: Upm 3B 40
Limes, The CM13: Bwood 6H 5
RM11: Horn 1B 24
Limes Av. E11 . . . . .2A 18
E12 .2C 26
IG7: Chig 2G 9
(not continuous)
Limes Ct. CM15: Bwood 4F 5
Limewood Ct. IG4: Ilf 3D 18
Lincoln Av. RM7: Rush G 1D 30
Lincoln Cl. RM11: Horn 3E 25
Lincoln Gdns. IG1: Ilf 5C 18
Lincoln Rd. E7 . . . . .5B 26
Linden Ri. CM14: War 2F 17
Linden St. RM7: Rom 2D 22
Lindfield Rd. RM3: Rom 2C 14
Lindisfarne Rd. RM8: Dag 2E 29
Lindsey Cl. CM14: Bwood 1C 16
Lindsey Rd. RM8: Dag 3E 29
Lindsey Way RM11: Horn 3A 24
Lingfield Av. RM14: Upm 2D 32
Link Pl. IG6: Ilf 3B 10
Link Rd. E12 . . . . .1C 26
RM9: Dag 2F 37
Links Av. RM2: Rom 6H 13
Linkside IG7: Chig 2G 9
Link Way RM11: Horn 6C 24
Linkway RM8: Dag 3E 29
Linkway Rd. CM14: Bwood 6B 4
Linley Cres. RM7: Mawney 1B 22
Linsdell Rd. IG11: Bark 1C 34
Linton Ct. RM1: Rom 6E 13
Linton Rd. IG11: Bark 6G 27
Lintons, The IG11: Bark 6G 27
Lion & Lamb Ct.
CM14: Bwood 5E 5
(off High St.)
Lion Rd. E6 . . . . .5A 34
Liphook Cl. RM12: Horn 3F 31
Lister Av. RM3: Hrld W 6B 14
Liston Way IG8: Wfd G 4A 8
Listowel Rd. RM10: Dag 2A 30
Lit. Aston Rd. RM3: Hrld W 4E 15
Lit. Gaynes Gdns.
RM14: Upm 3F 33
Lit. Gaynes La. RM14: Upm 3D 32
Little Gearies IG6: Ilf 2F 19
Lit. Gerpins La. RM14: Upm 1H 39
LITTLE HEATH 2D 20
Little Heath RM6: Chad H 2D 20
LITTLE HIGHWOOD HOSPITAL . . .3D 4
LITTLE ILFORD 4D 26
Lit. Ilford La. E12 . . . . .3D 26
Littlemoor Rd. IG1: Ilf 2H 27
Lit. Pastures CM14: Bwood 1B 16
Little Russets CM13: Hut 3E 7
LITTLE WARLEY 6G 17
Lit. Warley Hall La.
CM13: L War 6G 17
Livingstone Ter. RM13: Rain 1A 38
Lloyd Rd. RM9: Dag 5H 29
Locke Cl. RM13: Rain 5F 31
Lockwood Wlk. RM1: Rom 3E 23
Lodge Av. RM2: Rom 2G 23
RM8: Dag 5D 28
RM9: Dag 1G 35
LODGE AVENUE FLYOVER JUNC.
. . . . .1G 35
Lodge Cl. CM13: Hut 3E 7
IG7: Chig 1C 10
Lodge Ct. RM12: Horn 1C 32
Lodge Hill IG4: Ilf 2C 18
Lodge La. RM5: Col R 4A 12
Logan Ct. RM1: Rom 3E 23
Logan M. RM1: Rom 3E 23
Lombard Av. IG3: Ilf 6A 20
Lombard Ct. RM7: Rom 2C 22
Lombards, The RM11: Horn 5D 24
Lombardy Cl. IG6: Ilf 4F 9
London Ind. Pk., The
E6 .5B 34
(not continuous)
London Rd. CM14: Bwood 1B 16
IG11: Bark 6F 27
RM7: Chad H, Rom 4A 22
Londons Cl. RM14: Upm 4G 33
Longaford Way CM13: Hut 4C 6
Longbridge Ho. RM8: Dag 3D 28
(off Gainsborough Rd.)
Longbridge Rd. IG11: Bark 5H 27
RM8: Dag 3C 28
Longdon Ct. RM1: Rom 3F 23
Longfellow Dr. CM13: Hut 3C 6
Longfield Av. RM11: Horn 5F 23
Long Grn. IG7: Chig 1A 10
Long Gro. RM3: Hrld W 6C 14
Longhayes Av. RM6: Chad H 2F 21
Longhayes Ct. RM6: Chad H 2F 21
Longmead Cl. CM15: Shenf 4G 5
Long Mdw. CM13: Hut 5C 6
Longport Cl. IG6: Ilf 3C 10
Longreach Ct. IG11: Bark 2D 34
Long Reach Rd. IG11: Bark 4F 35
Longridge Rd. IG11: Bark 6G 27
Long Ridings Av. CM13: Hut 1B 6
Longtown Cl. RM3: Rom 2A 14
Longtown Rd. RM3: Rom 2A 14
Longview Vs. RM5: Col R 5H 11
Longview Way RM5: Col R 5D 12
Longwood Cl. RM14: Upm 4G 33
Longwood Ct. RM14: Upm 4G 33
(off Corbets Tey Rd.)
Longwood Gdns. IG5: Ilf 2D 18
IG6: Ilf 2D 18
Longworth Cl. SE28 . . . . .6B 36
Lonsdale Av. CM13: Hut 2D 6
E6 .4A 34
RM7: Rom 4C 22
Lonsdale Cres. IG2: Ilf 4F 19
Looe Gdns. IG6: Ilf 1F 19
Lord Av. IG5: Ilf 2D 18
Lord Ct. IG5: Ilf 2D 18
Lord Gdns. IG5: Ilf 2D 18
Lordship Cl. CM13: Hut 3D 6
Lorimar Bus. Cen.
RM13: Rain 5A 38
Lorne Gdns. E11 . . . . .2A 18
Lorne Rd. CM14: War 1E 17
E7 .3A 26
Loudoun Av. IG6: Ilf 3F 19
Louise Gdns. RM13: Rain 3A 38
Lovelace Gdns. IG11: Bark 3C 28
Loveland Mans. IG11: Bark 6B 28
(off Upney La.)
Love La. IG8: Wfd G 3D 8
Lovell Wlk. RM13: Rain 5G 31
Lovers Wlk. RM5: Have B 2D 12
Lowbrook Rd. IG1: Ilf 3F 27
Lowe, The IG7: Chig 1C 10
Lowe Cl. IG7: Chig 2C 10
Lowen Rd. RM13: Rain 2H 37
Lwr. Bedfords Rd.
RM1: Have B, Rom 3E 13
Lwr. Broad St. RM10: Dag 1E 37
Lwr. Mardyke Av. RM13: Rain 2G 37
Lowlands Gdns. RM7: Rom 4B 22
Lowry Rd. RM8: Dag 4D 28
Lowshoe La. RM5: Col R 5A 12
LOXFORD 4G 27
Loxford La. IG1: Ilf 4G 27
IG3: Ilf 3A 28
Loxford Rd. IG11: Bark 5F 27
Loxford Ter. IG11: Ilf 5G 27
Lucas Av. E13 . . . . .6A 26
Lucerne Way RM3: Rom 3B 14
Lucy Gdns. RM8: Dag 2H 29
Ludham Cl. IG6: Ilf 5G 9
SE28 . . . . .6A 36
Lugg App. E12 . . . . .2E 27
Lullington Rd. RM9: Dag 6G 29
Lulworth Dr. RM5: Col R 2B 12
Lumiere Bldg., The E7 . . . . .4B 26
(off Romford Rd.)
Lupin Cl. RM7: Rush G 1D 30
Lupin Cres. IG1: Ilf 5F 27
Luppits Cl. CM13: Hut 4A 6
Luton Ho. RM3: Rom 2C 14
(off Lindfield Rd.)
Luxborough La. IG7: Chig 1C 8
Lydeard Rd. E6 . . . . .6D 26
Lymington Rd. RM8: Dag 6F 21
Lynbrook Cl. RM13: Rain 2H 37
Lyndhurst Dr. RM11: Horn 6A 24
Lyndhurst Gdns. IG2: Ilf 4H 19
IG11: Bark 5A 28
Lyndhurst Ri. IG7: Chig 1E 9
Lyndhurst Way CM13: Hut 3C 6
Lynford Gdns. IG3: Ilf 1B 28
Lynmouth Ho. RM3: Rom 2C 14
(off Dagnam Pk. Dr.)
Lynnett Rd. RM8: Dag 1F 29
Lynn Rd. IG2: Ilf 5H 19
Lynross Cl. RM3: Hrld W 6D 14
Lynton Av. RM7: Mawney 5A 12
Lynton Cres. IG2: Ilf 4F 19
Lynton Ho. IG1: Ilf 1G 27
Lynwood Cl. E18 . . . . .5A 8
RM5: Col R 3B 12
Lynwood Dr. RM5: Col R 3B 12
Lyon Bus. Pk. IG11: Bark 2E 35
Lyon Rd. RM1: Rom 5F 23
Lytham Cl. SE28 . . . . .6C 36
Lytton Rd. RM2: Rom 3H 23
Lytton Ter. E12 . . . . .5D 26

M

Macclesfield Ho. RM3: Rom 2C 14
(off Dagnam Pk. Dr.)
Macdonald Av. RM10: Dag 2B 30
RM11: Horn 1C 24
Macdonald Way
RM11: Horn 2C 24
McIntosh Cl. RM1: Rom 1E 23
McIntosh Rd. RM1: Rom 1E 23
Maclennan Av. RM13: Rain 3F 39
Macon Way RM14: Upm 3A 40
Madeira Gro. IG8: Wfd G 3A 8
Madeira Wlk. CM15: Bwood 6G 5
Madeleine Cl. RM6: Chad H 4E 21
Madeline Gro. IG1: Ilf 4H 27
Madge Gill Way E6 . . . . .6C 26
(off High St. Nth.)
Madras Rd. IG1: Ilf 3F 27
Mafeking Av. IG2: Ilf 5H 19
Magdalene Gdns. E6 . . . . .4A 34
Magdalen Gdns.
CM13: Hut 2E 7
Magnolia Way CM15: Pil H 1D 4
Magnum Cl. RM13: Rain 4D 38
Magpie La. CM13: L War 6F 17
Maidstone Av. RM5: Col R 6C 12
Main Rd. RM1: Rom 2F 23
RM2: Rom 2F 23
Maizey Ct. CM15: Pil H 1C 4
Malan Sq. RM13: Rain 5H 31
Maldon Ct. E6 . . . . .1A 34
Maldon Rd. RM7: Rush G 5C 22
Maldon Wlk. IG8: Wfd G 3A 8
Mall, The RM10: Dag 5A 30
RM11: Horn 6H 23
(not continuous)
Mallard Cl. RM14: Upm 3B 40
Mallards Rd. IG8: Wfd G 4A 8
IG11: Bark 3G 35
Mallard Way CM13: Hut 3B 6
Mallinson Cl. RM12: Horn 4A 32
Malpas Rd. RM9: Dag 5F 29
Malt Ho. Pl. RM1: Rom 3E 23
Maltings, The RM1: Rom 5F 23
Malvern Dr. IG3: Bark, Ilf 3B 28
IG8: Wfd G 2A 8
Malvern Rd. E6 . . . . .6C 26
RM11: Horn 4G 23
Manbrough Av. E6 . . . . .3A 34
Manchester Way RM10: Dag 3B 30
Mandeville Wlk. CM13: Hut 3E 7
Manford Cl. IG7: Chig 1C 10
Manford Ct. IG7: Chig 2B 10
(off Manford Way)
Manford Cross IG7: Chig 2C 10
Manford Way IG7: Chig 2A 10
Manning Rd. RM10: Dag 5A 30
Mannin Rd. RM6: Chad H 5D 20
Mannock M. E18 . . . . .5A 8
Manor Av. E7 . . . . .3A 26
RM11: Horn 3A 24
Manor Cl. RM1: Rom 3G 23
RM10: Dag 5D 30
SE28 . . . . .6A 36
Manor Ct. IG11: Bark 6B 28
Manor Cres. RM11: Horn 3A 24
Manor Dene SE28 . . . . .6A 36
Manordene Rd. SE28 . . . . .6A 36
Mnr. Farm Ct. E6 . . . . .3A 34
MANOR PARK 3B 26
Manor Pk. Crematorium
E7 .3A 26
Manor Pk. Rd. E12 . . . . .3B 26
(not continuous)
Manor Park Station (Rail) 3B 26
Manor Rd. IG7: Chig 2G 9
IG8: Wfd G 3D 8
IG11: Bark 5B 28
RM1: Rom 3G 23
RM6: Chad H 4F 21
RM10: Dag 5C 30
Manor Sq. RM8: Dag 1E 29
Manor Way CM14: Bwood 6C 4
IG8: Wfd G 2A 8
RM13: Rain 4A 38
Manor Way Bus. Cen.
RM13: Rain 5H 37
Manpreet Ct. E12 . . . . .4D 26
Mansard Cl. RM12: Horn 1G 31
Manser Ct. RM13: Rain 3A 38
Manser Rd. RM13: Rain 3A 38
Mansfield Gdns. RM12: Horn 1B 32
Mansfield Rd. E11 . . . . .4A 18
IG1: Ilf 1E 27
Manstead Gdns. RM13: Rain . . .6D 38
Mansted Gdns. RM6: Chad H . . .5E 21
Manston Way RM12: Horn 5H 31
Maple Av. RM14: Upm 2F 33
Maple Cl. CM13: Bwood 6H 5
IG6: Ilf 2A 10
RM12: Horn 2H 31
Maple Ct. E6 . . . . .5A 34
Mapleleafe Gdns. IG6: Ilf 1F 19
Maplestead Rd. RM9: Dag 1H 35
Maple St. RM7: Rom 2C 22
Marabou Cl. E12 . . . . .4C 26
Marchmant Cl. RM12: Horn 2A 32
Marconi Gdns. CM15: Pil H 1E 5
Marden Rd. RM1: Rom 4E 23
Mardyke Cl. RM13: Rain 2G 37
Mardyke Ho. RM13: Rain 2H 37
Margaret Av. CM15: Shenf 3H 5
Margaret Bondfield Av.
IG11: Bark 6C 28
Margaret Cl. RM2: Rom 3H 23
Margaret Dr. RM11: Horn 6D 24
Margaret Rd. RM2: Rom 3H 23
Margaretting Rd. E12 . . . . .6A 18
Margaret Way IG4: Ilf 4C 18
Margery Rd. RM8: Dag 2F 29
Mariam Gdns. RM12: Horn 1D 32
Marian Lawson Ct.
IG7: Chig 2C 10
Marina Gdns. RM7: Rom 3B 22
Marine Dr. IG11: Bark 4G 35
Mariner Rd. E12 . . . . .3E 27
Marion Cl. IG6: Ilf 4H 9
Market Link RM1: Rom 2E 23
Market Pl. RM1: Rom 3E 23
Market St. E6 . . . . .2A 34
Markham Ho. RM10: Dag 2A 30
(off Uvedale Rd.)
MARKS GATE 5G 11
Marks Lodge RM7: Rom 3D 22
Marks Rd. RM7: Rom 3C 22
(not continuous)
Mark Wade Cl. E12 . . . . .6B 18
Markyate Rd. RM8: Dag 4D 28
Marlands Rd. IG5: Ilf 1C 18
Marlborough Cl. RM14: Upm 4A 40
Marlborough Dr. IG5: Ilf 1C 18
Marlborough Gdns.
RM14: Upm 6H 25
Marlborough Rd. CM15: Pil H 2C 4
E7 .6A 26
RM7: Mawney 2A 22
RM8: Dag 3D 28
Marlowe Cl. IG6: Ilf 5G 9
Marlowe Gdns. RM3: Rom 5A 14
Marlowe Ho. IG8: Wfd G 4E 9
Marlyon Rd. IG6: Ilf 2D 10
Marquis Ct. IG11: Bark 4A 28
Marshalls Dr. RM1: Rom 1E 23
Marshalls Rd. RM7: Rom 2D 22
Marsh Grn. Rd. RM10: Dag 1E 37
Marsh Way RM13: Dag, Rain 3H 37
Marston Av. RM10: Dag 1A 30
Marston Cl. RM10: Dag 2A 30
Marston Rd. IG5: Ilf 5C 8
Martham Cl. IG6: Ilf 5F 9
SE28 . . . . .6B 36
Martina Ter. IG7: Chig 2A 10
Martin Dr. RM13: Rain 4D 38
Martin Gdns. RM8: Dag 3E 29
Martin Rd. RM8: Dag 3E 29
Martinsfield Cl. IG7: Chig 1A 10
Martinstown Cl. RM11: Horn 4E 25
Martlesham Cl. RM12: Horn 4A 32
Martley Dr. IG2: Ilf 3F 19
Marwell Cl. RM1: Rom 3G 23

52 A-Z Romford

Perth Ter.—Riversdale Rd.

Perth Ter. IG2: Ilf 5G **19**
Petands Ct. *RM12: Horn 2B* ***32***
(off Randall Dr.)
Peterborough Av. RM14: Upm 4A **40**
Peterborough Gdns. IG1: Ilf 5C **18**
Peters Cl. RM8: Dag 6F **21**
Petersfield Av. RM3: Rom 3C **14**
Petersfield Cl. RM3: Rom 3E **15**
Pett Cl. RM11: Horn 1H **31**
Pettits Blvd. RM1: Rom 5E **13**
Pettits Cl. RM1: Rom 6E **13**
Pettits La. RM1: Rom 6E **13**
Pettits La. Nth. RM1: Rom 5D **12**
Pettits Pl. RM10: Dag 4A **30**
Pettits Rd. RM10: Dag 4A **30**
Pettley Gdns. RM7: Rom 3D **22**
Petworth Way RM12: Horn 3F **31**
Peverel E6 6A **34**
Peverel Ho. RM10: Dag 1A **30**
Philan Way RM5: Col R 3D **12**
Philip Av. RM7: Rush G 6D **22**
Philip Cl. CM15: Pil H 2D **4**
RM7: Rush G 6D **22**
Philip Rd. RM13: Rain 3A **38**
Phillida Rd. RM3: Hrld W 6E **15**
Philpot Path IG1: Ilf 2G **27**
Pickering Av. E6 2A **34**
Pike La. RM14: Upm 6B **40**
Pilgrim's Cl. CM15: Pil H 1B **4**
PILGRIMS HATCH 2D **4**
Pilgrims La. CM14: Pil H 1A **4**
Pimpernel Way RM3: Rom 3B **14**
Pinecourt RM14: Upm 3F **33**
Pine Cres. CM13: Hut 1D **6**
Pinecroft CM13: Hut 3B **6**
RM2: Rom 2A **24**
Pinewood Av. RM13: Rain 4D **38**
Pinewood Rd. RM4: Have B 1C **12**
Pinewood Way CM13: Hut 1D **6**
Pinley Gdns. RM9: Dag 1H **35**
Pintail Rd. IG8: Wfd G 4A **8**
Pioneer Mkt. *IG1: Ilf 2F* ***27***
(off Winston Way)
Pitcairn Cl. RM7: Mawney 2A **22**
Pittman Gdns. IG1: Ilf 4G **27**
Pittwood CM15: Shenf 4A **6**
Plantagenet Gdns.
RM6: Chad H 5F **21**
Plantagenet Pl. RM6: Chad H 5F **21**
PLASHET 5C **26**
Plashet Gdns. CM13: Bwood 6A **6**
Plashet Gro. E6 6A **26**
Platford Grn. RM11: Horn 2C **24**
Playfield Av. RM5: Col R 5C **12**
Plough Ri. RM14: Upm 3A **40**
Plover Gdns. RM14: Upm 4B **40**
Plowman Way RM8: Dag 6E **21**
Plumpton Av. RM12: Horn 3C **32**
Plumtree Cl. RM10: Dag 5B **30**
Plymouth Ho. *IG11: Bark 6C* ***28***
(off Keir Hardie Way)
Pointer Cl. SE28 6B **36**
Polesworth Rd. RM9: Dag 6F **29**
Pollard Cl. IG7: Chig 2C **10**
Pompadour Cl. CM14: War 2E **17**
Pondfield La. CM13: Bwood 6A **6**
Pondfield Rd. RM10: Dag 4B **30**
Pond Lees Cl. RM10: Dag 6D **30**
Pond Wlk. RM14: Upm 5A **40**
Pontypool Wlk. RM3: Rom 3A **14**
Poole Rd. RM11: Horn 5D **24**
Poplar Dr. CM13: Hut 2C **6**
Poplar Gdns. SE28 6A **36**
Poplar Rd. E12 1C **26**
Poplar St. RM7: Rom 2C **22**
Poplar Way IG6: Ilf 2G **19**
Poppy Cl. CM15: Pil H 1D **4**
Porchester Cl. RM11: Horn 4C **24**
Porter Rd. E6 6A **34**
Porters Av. RM8: Dag 5D **28**
RM9: Dag 5D **28**
Porters Cl. CM14: Bwood 4C **4**
Portia Ct. IG11: Bark 6C **28**
Portland Cl. RM6: Chad H 3G **21**
Portland Commercial Est.
IG11: Bark 2A **36**
Portland Gdns. RM6: Chad H 3F **21**
Portmadoc Ho. *RM3: Rom 1C* ***14***
(off Broseley Rd.)
Portman Dr. IG8: Wfd G 6B **8**
Portmore Gdns. RM5: Col R 2A **12**
Portnoi Cl. RM1: Rom 6D **12**
Portway RM13: Rain 1C **38**
Postway M. IG1: Ilf 2F **27**
(not continuous)
Potiphar Pl. CM14: War 1D **16**
Poulett Rd. E6 2A **34**
Powell Gdns. RM10: Dag 3A **30**
Powerleague Soccer Cen.
Barking 3C **34**
Fairlop 4B **10**
Pownsett Ter. IG1: Ilf 4G **27**
Poynings Way RM3: Hrld W 5C **14**
Prestbury Rd. E7 6A **26**
Preston Dr. E11 3A **18**
Preston Gdns. IG1: Ilf 4C **18**
Preston Ho. *RM10: Dag 2A* ***30***
(off Uvedale Rd.)
Preston Rd. RM3: Rom 1B **14**
Prestwood Dr. RM5: Col R 2C **12**
Pretoria Rd. IG1: Ilf 4F **27**
RM7: Rom 2C **22**
Priestley Gdns. RM6: Chad H 4D **20**
Priests Av. RM1: Rom 6D **12**
Priests La.
CM15: Bwood, Shenf 3H **5**
Primrose Av. RM6: Chad H 5D **20**
Primrose Ct. CM14: Bwood 6E **5**
Primrose Glen RM11: Horn 2C **24**
Primrose Hill CM14: Bwood 6E **5**
Princes Av. IG8: Wfd G 1A **8**
Princes Pk. RM13: Rain 6G **31**
Princes Rd. IG6: Ilf 2H **19**
RM1: Rom 3G **23**
Princess Cl. SE28 6B **36**
Princess Pde. RM10: Dag 2E **37**
Princes Way CM13: Hut 5A **6**
Prior Rd. IG1: Ilf 2E **27**
Priors Pk. RM12: Horn 2A **32**
Priory Cl. CM15: Pil H 1C **4**
Priory Gro. RM3: Rom 1C **14**
Priory M. RM11: Horn 6H **23**
Priory Path RM3: Rom 1C **14**
Priory Rd. IG11: Bark 6H **27**
RM3: Rom 1C **14**
Prospect Pl. RM5: Col R 6C **12**
Prospect Rd. IG8: Wfd G 3A **8**
RM11: Horn 1D **24**
Prospect Way CM13: Hut 1E **7**
Providence Pl. RM5: Col R 5H **11**
Puffin Cl. IG11: Bark 3H **35**
Pulborough Ho. *RM3: Rom 4C* ***14***
(off Kingsbridge Cir.)
Purbeck Rd. RM11: Horn 5G **23**
Purland Cl. RM8: Dag 6H **21**
Purleigh Av. IG8: Wfd G 3C **8**
Purley Cl. IG5: Ilf 6E **9**
Putney Gdns. RM6: Chad H 3D **20**

Q

Quadrant Arc. RM1: Rom 3E **23**
Quakers Pl. E7 4B **26**
Quarles Cl. RM5: Col R 4A **12**
Quebec Rd. IG1: Ilf 5F **19**
IG2: Ilf 5F **19**
Queenborough Gdns. IG2: Ilf 2E **19**
Queen Mary Cl. RM1: Rom 4F **23**
Queen's Av. IG8: Wfd G 2A **8**
Queensberry Pl. E12 4B **26**
Queens Gdns. RM13: Rain 2H **37**
RM14: Upm 2B **40**
Queen's Pk. Rd.
RM3: Hrld W 5E **15**
Queens Rd. CM14: Bwood 6E **5**
IG11: Bark 5G **27**
Queens Theatre
Hornchurch 5B **24**
Queenstown Gdns.
RM13: Rain 3B **38**
Queen St. CM14: War 2E **17**
RM7: Rom 4D **22**
Queenswood Av. CM13: Hut 1D **6**
Queenswood Ho. *CM14: Bwood 5F* ***5***
(off Eastfield Rd.)
Quennell Way CM13: Hut 3C **6**

R

Rabbits Rd. E12 3C **26**
Rachel Cl. IG6: Ilf 1H **19**
Radford Way IG11: Bark 3F **35**
Radley Av. IG3: Bark, Ilf 3C **28**
Radleys Mead RM10: Dag 5B **30**
Radnor Cres. IG4: Ilf 3D **18**
Radstock Ho. *RM3: Rom 2B* ***14***
(off Darlington Gdns.)
Raider Cl. RM7: Mawney 5A **12**
Railway Pde. *CM15: Shenf 3A* ***6***
(off Hutton Rd.)
Railway Sq. CM14: Bwood 6E **5**
Railway St. RM6: Chad H 5E **21**
RAINHAM 4C **38**
Rainham Hall 4C **38**
Rainham Rd.
RM12: Horn, Rain 4F **31**
RM13: Rain 3C **38**
Rainham Rd. Nth. RM10: Dag 1A **30**
Rainham Rd. Sth. RM10: Dag 3B **30**
Rainham Station (Rail)
Essex 4C **38**
Rainham Trad. Est.
RM13: Rain 4B **38**
Rainsford Way RM12: Horn 6G **23**
Ramsay Gdns. RM3: Rom 5A **14**
Ramsden Dr. RM5: Col R 4A **12**
Ramsgill App. IG2: Ilf 2B **20**
Ramsgill Dr. IG2: Ilf 3B **20**
Rams Gro. RM6: Chad H 2G **21**
Randall Ct. RM13: Rain 4D **38**
Randall Dr. RM12: Horn 3A **32**
Randalls Dr. CM13: Hut 2E **7**
Randolph Gro. RM6: Chad H 3E **21**
Ranelagh Gdns. E11 3A **18**
IG1: Ilf 6D **18**
Ranelagh Rd. E6 1A **34**
Raphael Av. RM1: Rom 1F **23**
Ratcliff Rd. E7 4A **26**
Ravenings Pde. IG3: Ilf 6C **20**
Ravenoak Way IG7: Chig 2A **10**
Raven Rd. E18 6A **8**
Ravensbourne Cres.
RM3: Hrld W 1D **24**
Ravensbourne Gdns. IG5: Ilf 5E **9**
Ravenscourt CM15: Bwood 3E **5**
Ravenscourt Cl. RM12: Horn 2C **32**
Ravenscourt Dr. RM12: Horn 2C **32**
Ravenscourt Gro.
RM12: Horn 1C **32**
Ravensfield Cl. RM9: Dag 3F **29**
Ravenswood Cl. RM5: Col R 2B **12**
Rayburn Rd. RM11: Horn 5E **25**
Raydons Gdns. RM9: Dag 3G **29**
Raydons Rd. RM9: Dag 4G **29**
Ray Gdns. IG11: Bark 2G **35**
Rayleigh Cl. CM13: Hut 2C **6**
Rayleigh Rd. CM13: Hut 2B **6**
IG8: Wfd G 3A **8**
Ray Lodge Rd. IG8: Wfd G 3A **8**
Ray Massey Way *E6 6C* ***26***
(off High St. Nth.)
Raymond Rd. E13 6A **26**
IG2: Ilf 5H **19**
Raynes Av. E11 5A **18**
Ray Rd. RM5: Col R 2B **12**
Reads Cl. IG1: Ilf 2F **27**
Recreation Av. RM3: Hrld W 6D **14**
RM7: Rom 3C **22**
Rectory Cres. E11 4A **18**
(not continuous)
Rectory Gdns. RM14: Upm 1H **33**
Rectory Rd. E12 4D **26**
RM10: Dag 5B **30**
Redbourne Dr. SE28 6B **36**
(not continuous)
REDBRIDGE 4C **18**
Redbridge Ent. Cen. IG1: Ilf 1G **27**
Redbridge FC 2H **19**
Redbridge Foyer *IG1: Ilf 1G* ***27***
(off Sylvan Rd.)
Redbridge La. E. IG4: Ilf 4B **18**
Redbridge La. W. E11 4A **18**
REDBRIDGE RDBT. 4B **18**
Redbridge Sports Cen. 5H **9**
Redbridge Station (Tube) 4B **18**
Redbury Cl. RM13: Rain 4E **39**
Redcar Rd. RM3: Rom 2D **14**
Redcliffe Gdns. IG1: Ilf 6E **19**
Redden Ct. RM3: Hrld W 6D **14**
Redden Ct. Rd. RM3: Hrld W 1C **24**
Redfern Gdns. RM2: Rom 6B **14**
Redif Ho. RM10: Dag 3B **30**
Redo Ho. *E12 4E* ***27***
(off Dore Av.)
Red Post Ho. E6 6B **26**
Redriff Rd. RM7: Mawney 6B **12**
Red Rd. CM14: War 1D **16**
Redruth Gdns. RM3: Rom 2D **14**
Redruth Rd. RM3: Rom 2D **14**
Redruth Wlk. RM3: Rom 2D **14**
Redwing Ct. RM3: Rom 5B **14**
Redwood Gdns. IG7: Chig 2C **10**
Reede Gdns. RM10: Dag 4B **30**
Reede Rd. RM10: Dag 5A **30**
Reede Way RM10: Dag 5B **30**
Reed Pond Wlk. RM2: Rom 6F **13**
Reesland Cl. E12 5E **27**
Regarder Rd. IG7: Chig, Ilf 2C **10**
Regarth Av. RM1: Rom 4E **23**
Regency Cl. IG7: Chig 2G **9**
Regency Ct. CM14: Bwood 5E **5**
Regency Gdns. RM11: Horn 5A **24**
Regent Gdns. IG3: Ilf 5C **20**
Regent Ho. CM14: Bwood 6D **4**
Regents Dr. IG8: Wfd G 3E **9**
Reginald Rd. RM3: Hrld W 5E **15**
Reigate Rd. IG3: Ilf 1B **28**
Remembrance Rd. E7 3B **26**
Renfrew Cl. E6 6A **34**
Renown Cl. RM7: Mawney 5A **12**
Renwick Ind. Est. IG11: Bark 2H **35**
Renwick Rd. IG11: Bark 4H **35**
Repton Av. RM2: Rom 1G **23**
Repton Ct. IG5: Ilf 5D **8**
Repton Dr. RM2: Rom 2G **23**
Repton Gdns. RM2: Rom 1G **23**
Repton Gro. IG5: Ilf 5D **8**
REPTON PARK 4E **9**
Repulse Cl. RM5: Col R 5A **12**
Retford Cl. RM3: Rom 3E **15**
Retford Path RM3: Rom 3E **15**
Retford Rd. RM3: Rom 3D **14**
Retreat, The CM13: Hut 2B **6**
CM14: Bwood 4D **4**
Reubens Rd. CM13: Hut 2B **6**
Review Rd. RM10: Dag 1F **37**
Rex Cl. RM5: Col R 4B **12**
Reydon Av. E11 3A **18**
Reynolds Av. E12 4E **27**
RM6: Chad H 5E **21**
Reynolds Ct. RM6: Chad H 1F **21**
Rhapsody Cres. CM14: War 1D **16**
Ribble Cl. IG8: Wfd G 3A **8**
Richard Blackburn Ho.
RM7: Rush G 1E **31**
Richard Fell Ho. *E12 3E* ***27***
(off Walton Rd.)
Richards Av. RM7: Rom 4C **22**
Richardson Gdns. RM10: Dag 5B **30**
Riches Rd. IG1: Ilf 1G **27**
Richmond Dr. IG8: Ilf 4E **9**
Richmond Rd. E7 4A **26**
(not continuous)
IG1: Ilf 2G **27**
RM1: Rom 4F **23**
Ridgemont Pl. RM11: Horn 4B **24**
Ridge Way IG8: Wfd G 1A **8**
Ridgeway CM13: Hut 4B **6**
Ridgeway, The RM2: Rom 2G **23**
RM3: Hrld W 5D **14**
Ridgeway Gdns. IG4: Ilf 3C **18**
Ridgewell Cl. RM10: Dag 1F **37**
Ridgewell Gro. RM12: Horn 6H **31**
Ridings, The IG7: Chig 1D **10**
Ridley Cl. IG11: Bark 6B **28**
RM3: Rom 5H **13**
Ridley Rd. E7 3A **26**
Riffhams CM13: Bwood 6B **6**
Rigby M. IG1: Ilf 1E **27**
Ringles Ct. E6 1A **34**
Ringwood Av. RM12: Horn 1B **32**
Ripley Rd. IG3: Ilf 1B **28**
Ripon Gdns. IG1: Ilf 4C **18**
Ripon Ho. *RM3: Rom 3B* ***14***
(off Dartfields)
Ripple Nature Reserve, The 3H **35**
Ripple Rd. IG11: Bark, Dag 6G **27**
RM9: Dag 1H **35**
RIPPLESIDE 1H **35**
Rippleside Commercial Est.
IG11: Bark 2A **36**
Risebridge Chase RM1: Rom 4F **13**
Risebridge Rd. RM2: Rom 6F **13**
RISE PARK 6E **13**
Rise Pk. Blvd. RM1: Rom 5F **13**
Rise Pk. Pde. RM1: Rom 6E **13**
Riseway CM15: Bwood 6G **5**
Risings Ter. *RM11: Horn 1D* ***24***
(off Prospect Rd.)
River Cl. E11 4A **18**
RM13: Rain 5D **38**
Riverdale Cl. IG11: Bark 4H **35**
Riverdene Rd. IG1: Ilf 2E **27**
River Dr. RM14: Upm 4G **25**
River Rd. CM14: Bwood 1B **16**
IG11: Bark 2E **35**
River Rd. Bus. Pk. IG11: Bark 3F **35**
Riversdale Rd. RM5: Col R 4B **12**

Riverside Cotts.—Sebert Rd.

Riverside Cotts. IG11: Bark 2D **34**
Riverside Ind. Est. IG11: Bark 3G **35**
Riverside Works IG11: Bark 6F **27**
Rivington Av. IG8: Wfd G 6B **8**
Rixsen Rd. E12 4C **26**
Robert Cl. IG7: Chig 2B **10**
Roberts Cl. RM3: Rom 5H **13**
Robin Cl. RM5: Col R 4D **12**
Robin Hood Rd. CM15: Bwood 3D **4**
Robinia Cl. IG6: Ilf 2A **10**
Robinson Cl. RM12: Horn 6H **31**
Robinson Rd. RM10: Dag 3A **30**
Roborough Wlk. RM12: Horn 5A **32**
Rochester Gdns. IG1: Ilf 5D **18**
Rochester Rd. RM12: Horn 6H **31**
Rochford Av. CM15: Shenf 1A **6**
RM6: Chad H 3E **21**
Rochford Cl. RM12: Horn 5H **31**
Rockchase Gdns.
RM11: Horn 4C **24**
Rock Gdns. RM10: Dag 4B **30**
Rockingham Av. RM11: Horn 4H **23**
Rockleigh Ct. CM15: Shenf 3A **6**
Rockwell Rd. RM10: Dag 4B **30**
Roden St. IG1: Ilf 2E **27**
Roden Way *IG1: Ilf 2E **27***
(off Roden St.)
Roding CM14: Bwood 4D **4**
Roding Av. IG8: Wfd G 3C **8**
RODING BUPA HOSPITAL 1B **18**
Roding La. Nth. IG8: Wfd G 3C **8**
Roding La. Sth.
IG4: Ilf, Wfd G 2B **18**
IG8: Wfd G 1B **18**
Roding Rd. E6 5B **34**
Rodings, The IG8: Wfd G 3A **8**
RM14: Upm 4H **25**
Roding Trad. Est. IG11: Bark 6F **27**
Roding Valley Station (Tube) 1B **8**
Roding Way RM13: Rain 2F **39**
Rodney Rd. E11 2A **18**
Rodney Way RM7: Mawney 5B **12**
Roebuck Rd. IG6: Ilf 2D **10**
Roebuck Rd. Trad. Est.
IG6: Ilf 3D **10**
Roedean Dr. RM1: Rom 2E **23**
Roger Reede's Almshouses
RM1: Rom 2E **23**
Rogers Gdns. RM10: Dag 4A **30**
Roger's Ho. RM10: Dag 2A **30**
Rogers Rd. RM10: Dag 4A **30**
Roles Gro. RM6: Chad H 2F **21**
Rollesby Way SE28 6A **36**
Roll Gdns. IG2: Ilf 3E **19**
Roman Cl. RM13: Rain 2H **37**
Roman Ho. RM13: Rain 2H **37**
Roman Rd. E6 4A **34**
IG1: Ilf 5F **27**
Rom Cres. RM7: Rush G 5F **23**
ROMFORD 3F **23**
Romford Rd. E7 4A **26**
E12 4A **26**
IG7: Chad H, Chig 1D **10**
RM5: Col R 4G **11**
Romford Stadium (Greyhound)
4C **22**
Romford Station (Rail) 4E **23**
Romney Chase RM11: Horn 4D **24**
Romsey Gdns. RM9: Dag 1B **36**
Romsey Rd. RM9: Dag 1B **36**
Romside Pl. RM7: Rom 2D **22**
Rom Valley Way
RM7: Rush G 4E **23**
Ronald Rd. RM3: Hrld W 5E **15**
Roneo Cnr. RM12: Rom 6F **23**
Roneo Link RM12: Horn 6F **23**
Ron Leighton Way E6 6C **26**
Ronnie La. E12 3E **27**
Rook Cl. RM12: Rain 6G **31**
Rookery Cres. RM10: Dag 6B **30**
Rookwood Ho. IG11: Bark 2D **34**
Roosevelt Way RM10: Dag 5D **30**
Rosalind Ct. *IG11: Bark 6C **28***
(off Meadow Rd.)
Roseacre Cl. RM11: Horn 6D **24**
Rose Av. E18 6A **8**
Rose Bank CM14: Bwood 6F **5**
Rosebank Av. RM12: Horn 4A **32**
Roseberry Cl. RM14: Upm 2B **40**
Roseberry Gdns. RM14: Upm 2A **40**
Rosebery Av. E12 5C **26**
Rosebury Ct. CM13: Hut 2D **6**
Rosebury Sq. IG8: Ilf 4E **9**
Rosedale Dr. RM9: Dag 6D **28**
Rosedale Gdns. RM9: Dag 6D **28**
Rosedale Rd. E7 4A **26**
RM1: Col R 6C **12**
RM9: Dag 6D **28**
Rosedene Gdns. IG2: Ilf 2E **19**
Rose Glen RM7: Rush G 6E **23**
Rose Hatch Av. RM6: Chad H 1F **21**
Rose La. RM6: Chad H 1F **21**
Rosemary Av. RM1: Rom 1F **23**
Rosemary Dr. IG4: Ilf 3B **18**
Rosemary Gdns. RM8: Dag 6H **21**
Rosemead Gdns. CM13: Hut 1D **6**
Rosemount Cl. IG8: Wfd G 3D **8**
Rosepark Ct. IG5: Ilf 6D **8**
Rose Tree M. IG8: Wfd G 3C **8**
Rosetti Ter. *RM8: Dag 3D **28***
(off Marlborough Rd.)
Rose Valley CM14: Bwood 6E **5**
Rosewood Av. RM12: Horn 4G **31**
Rosewood Ct. RM6: Chad H 3E **21**
Roslyn Gdns. RM2: Rom 6F **13**
Rossall Cl. RM11: Horn 4G **23**
Ross Av. RM8: Dag 1H **29**
Rosslyn Av. RM3: Hrld W 6C **14**
RM8: Dag 5H **21**
Rosslyn Rd. IG11: Bark 6H **27**
Rothbury Av. RM13: Rain 5D **38**
Roth Dr. CM13: Hut 5B **6**
Rothsay Rd. E7 6A **26**
Rothwell Gdns. RM9: Dag 6E **29**
Rothwell Rd. RM9: Dag 1A **36**
Rotunda, The *RM7: Rom 3D **22***
(off Yew Tree Gdns.)
Roundaway Rd. IG5: Ilf 5D **8**
Round House, The
Havering-Atte-Bower 1F **13**
Roundwood Av. CM13: Hut 4A **6**
Roundwood Gro. CM13: Hut 3B **6**
Routh St. E6 5A **34**
Rover Av. IG6: Ilf 3B **10**
Rowallen Pde. RM8: Dag 6E **21**
Rowan Cl. IG1: Ilf 4H **27**
Rowan Grn. E. CM13: Bwood 1H **17**
Rowan Grn. W. CM13: Bwood 6H **5**
Rowan Wlk. RM11: Horn 2B **24**
Rowan Way RM6: Chad H 1E **21**
Rowdowns Rd. RM9: Dag 1D **36**
Rowe Gdns. IG11: Bark 2F **35**
Rowhedge CM13: Bwood 6A **6**
Rowland Cres. IG7: Chig 1A **10**
Rowlands Rd. RM8: Dag 1H **29**
Rowney Gdns. RM9: Dag 5E **29**
Rowney Rd. RM9: Dag 5D **28**
Roxburgh Av. RM14: Upm 2G **33**
Roxwell Gdns. CM13: Hut 1C **6**
Roxwell Rd. IG11: Bark 2G **35**
Roxwell Way IG8: Wfd G 4A **8**
Roxy Av. RM6: Chad H 5E **21**
Royal Cl. IG3: Ilf 5C **20**
Royal Cres. IG2: Ilf 4H **19**
Royal Docks Rd. E6 6B **34**
IG11: Bark 6B **34**
Royal Jubilee Ct. RM2: Rom 1G **23**
Royal Pde. *RM10: Dag 5B **30***
(off Church St.)
Roycraft Av. IG11: Bark 2F **35**
Roycroft Cl. E18 5A **8**
Roy Gdns. IG2: Ilf 2A **20**
Royle Cl. RM2: Rom 3H **23**
Royston Gdns. IG1: Ilf 4B **18**
Royston Pde. IG1: Ilf 4B **18**
Royston Rd. RM3: Hrld W 4E **15**
Rudyard Ct. CM14: War 2D **16**
Rugby Gdns. RM9: Dag 5E **29**
Rugby Rd. RM9: Dag 5D **28**
Rumford Shop. Hall
*RM1: Rom 2E **23***
(off Market Pl.)
Runcorn Ho. *RM3: Rom 3C **14***
(off Kingsbridge Cir.)
Running Waters CM13: Bwood 6A **6**
(not continuous)
Rural Cl. RM11: Horn 6H **23**
Rushdene Rd. CM15: Bwood 2E **5**
Rushden Gdns. IG5: Ilf 6E **9**
Rushdon Cl. RM1: Rom 3G **23**
RUSH GREEN 6D **22**
Rush Grn. Gdns.
RM7: Rush G 6C **22**
Rush Grn. Rd. RM7: Rush G 6B **22**
Rushmere Av. RM14: Upm 2G **33**
Rusholme Av. RM10: Dag 2A **30**
Ruskin Av. E12 5C **26**
RM14: Upm 5G **25**
Ruskin Gdns. RM3: Rom 4H **13**
Rusper Rd. RM9: Dag 5E **29**
Russell Cl. CM15: Bwood 3D **4**
Russell Gdns. IG2: Ilf 5H **19**
Russell Wilson Ho.
RM3: Hrld W 5D **14**
Russetts RM11: Horn 2C **24**
Rustic Cl. RM14: Upm 4A **40**
Rutland App. RM11: Horn 3E **25**
Rutland Dr. RM11: Horn 3E **25**
Rutland Gdns. RM8: Dag 4E **29**
Rutland Rd. E7 6B **26**
E11 3A **18**
IG1: Ilf 2F **27**
Rutley Cl. RM3: Hrld W 6B **14**
Ryder Gdns. RM13: Rain 5F **31**
Rye Cl. RM12: Horn 3A **32**
Ryecroft Av. IG5: Ilf 6F **9**

S

Sackville Cres. RM3: Hrld W 5C **14**
Sackville Gdns. IG1: Ilf 6D **18**
Saddleworth Rd. RM3: Rom 3A **14**
Saddleworth Sq. RM3: Rom 3A **14**
Saffron Rd. RM5: Col R 6D **12**
St Aidans Ct. IG11: Bark 2H **35**
St Alban's Av. E6 3A **34**
RM14: Upm 5A **40**
St Albans Rd. IG3: Ilf 6B **20**
St Andrew's Av. RM12: Horn 4F **31**
St Andrews Cl. SE28 6B **36**
St Andrew's Pl. CM15: Shenf 5H **5**
St Andrews Rd. E12 1C **26**
IG1: Ilf 5D **18**
RM7: Rom 4D **22**
St Annes Ter. IG6: Ilf 2A **10**
St Ann's IG11: Bark 1C **34**
St Ann's Rd. IG11: Bark 1C **34**
St Anthony's Av. IG8: Wfd G 3A **8**
St Awdry's Rd. IG11: Bark 6H **27**
St Awdry's Wlk. IG11: Bark 6G **27**
St Barnabas Rd. IG8: Wfd G 5A **8**
St Chad's Gdns. RM6: Chad H 5G **21**
St Chad's Rd. RM6: Chad H 5G **21**
St Charles Rd. CM14: Bwood 4D **4**
St Clair Cl. IG5: Ilf 6D **8**
St Dionis Rd. E12 2C **26**
St Dunstan's Rd. E7 5A **26**
St Edmund's Rd. IG1: Ilf 4D **18**
St Edwards Way RM1: Rom 3D **22**
St Erkenwald M. IG11: Bark 1D **34**
St Erkenwald Rd. IG11: Bark 1D **34**
St Ethelburga Ct.
RM3: Hrld W 6E **15**
ST FRANCIS HOSPICE 1E **13**
St Francis Way IG1: Ilf 3H **27**
St Gabriel's Cl. E11 6A **18**
St George's Av. E7 6A **26**
RM11: Horn 5D **24**
St Georges Cl. SE28 6B **36**
St George's Ct. CM14: Bwood 3D **4**
ST GEORGES HOSPITAL
(HORNCHURCH) 4C **32**
St George's Rd. E7 5A **26**
IG1: Ilf 5D **18**
RM9: Dag 4G **29**
St George's Sq. E7 6A **26**
St Giles Av. RM10: Dag 6B **30**
St Giles Cl. RM10: Dag 6B **30**
St Helen's Ct. RM13: Rain 4C **38**
St Helen's Rd. IG1: Ilf 4D **18**
St Ives Cl. RM3: Rom 4D **14**
St Ivian's Dr. RM2: Rom 1G **23**
St James Ct. E12 1A **26**
RM1: Rom 2F **23**
St James Gdns. RM6: Ilf 2D **20**
St James Ho. *RM1: Rom 3F **23***
(off Eastern Rd.)
St James's Rd. CM14: Bwood 6E **5**
St John's Av. CM14: War 1F **17**
St John's Cl. RM13: Rain 6G **31**
St Johns Rd. IG2: Ilf 5H **19**
IG11: Bark 1E **35**
RM5: Col R 2C **12**
St John's Ter. E7 5A **26**
St Kathryn's Pl. RM14: Upm 1G **33**
St Kilda's Rd. CM15: Bwood 3D **4**
St Lawrence Rd. RM14: Upm 1G **33**
St Leonard's Gdns. IG1: Ilf 4G **27**
ST LEONARDS HAMLET 6H **23**
St Leonards Way RM11: Horn 1H **31**
St Luke's Av. IG1: Ilf 4F **27**
St Luke's Path IG1: Ilf 4F **27**
St Margaret's IG11: Bark 1D **34**
St Margaret's Rd. E12 1A **26**
St Martin's Cl. CM13: Hut 5C **6**
St Mary's IG11: Bark 1D **34**
St Mary's App. E12 4D **26**
St Mary's Av. CM15: Shenf 1A **6**
E11 5A **18**
St Mary's La. RM14: Upm 1E **33**
St Mary's Rd. IG1: Ilf 1G **27**
St Mary's Way IG7: Chig 2E **9**
St Matthew's Cl. RM13: Rain 6G **31**
St Mellion Cl. SE28 6B **36**
St Neot's Rd. RM3: Rom 4D **14**
St Nicholas Av. RM12: Horn 2G **31**
St Olave's Rd. E6 1A **34**
St Paul's Rd. IG11: Bark 1C **34**
St Peter's Cl. IG2: Ilf 2A **20**
St Peter's Rd. CM14: War 1D **16**
Saints Dr. E7 4B **26**
St Stephen's Cres.
CM13: Bwood 6A **6**
St Stephens Pde. E7 6A **26**
St Stephen's Rd. E6 6A **26**
St Thomas Gdns. IG1: Ilf 5G **27**
St Thomas' Rd. CM14: Bwood 5F **5**
St Winefride's Av. E12 4D **26**
St Winifred's Cl. IG7: Chig 2G **9**
Salamons Way RM13: Rain 6A **38**
Salcombe Dr. RM6: Chad H 4H **21**
Salhouse Cl. SE28 6A **36**
Salisbury Av. IG11: Bark 6H **27**
Salisbury Cl. RM14: Upm 5A **40**
Salisbury Rd. E12 4B **26**
IG3: Ilf 1A **28**
RM2: Rom 3H **23**
RM10: Dag 5B **30**
Sally Murray Cl. E12 3E **27**
Saltash Rd. IG6: Ilf 4H **9**
Sandgate Cl. RM7: Rush G 5C **22**
Sandhurst Dr. IG3: Bark, Ilf 3B **28**
Sandown Av. RM10: Dag 5C **30**
RM12: Horn 1B **32**
Sandpiper Ter. IG5: Ilf 1F **19**
Sandpit La.
CM14: Pil H, S Weald 4B **4**
CM15: Pil H 4B **4**
Sandringham Cl. IG6: Ilf 1G **19**
Sandringham Gdns. IG6: Ilf 1G **19**
Sandringham Rd.
CM15: Pil H 2D **4**
E7 4A **26**
IG11: Bark 4B **28**
Sands Way IG8: Wfd G 3D **8**
Sandyhill Rd. IG1: Ilf 3F **27**
Sapphire Cl. E6 6A **34**
RM8: Dag 6E **21**
Sarre Av. RM12: Horn 5A **32**
Saunton Rd. RM12: Horn 1G **31**
Savage Gdns. E6 6A **34**
Saville Rd. RM6: Chad H 4H **21**
Sawyers Cl. RM10: Dag 5C **30**
Sawyers Ct. CM15: Shenf 3H **5**
Sawyers Gro. CM15: Bwood 4F **5**
Sawyers Hall La.
CM15: Bwood 3E **5**
Saxham Rd. IG11: Bark 2E **35**
Saxon Cl. CM13: Bwood 6A **6**
RM3: Hrld W 6D **14**
Saxon Rd. IG1: Ilf 5F **27**
Scholars Ct. *RM2: Rom 3H **23***
(off Academy Fields Rd.)
Scholars Way RM2: Rom 3H **23**
School La. IG7: Chig 1B **10**
School Rd. E12 3D **26**
RM10: Dag 1E **37**
School Way RM8: Dag 2E **29**
(not continuous)
Schooner Cl. IG11: Bark 3H **35**
Scoter Cl. IG8: Wfd G 4A **8**
Scotney Wlk. RM12: Horn 4A **32**
Scottes La. RM8: Dag 6F **21**
Scott Ho. *RM11: Horn 4G **23***
(off Benjamin Cl.)
Scotts Cl. RM12: Horn 4A **32**
Scrattons Ter. IG11: Bark 2B **36**
Seabrook Gdns.
RM7: Rush G 5A **22**
Seabrook Rd. RM8: Dag 2F **29**
Seaburn Cl. RM13: Rain 2A **38**
Seaforth Cl. RM1: Rom 4E **13**
Seaforth Gdns. IG8: Wfd G 2A **8**
Seagull Cl. IG11: Bark 3G **35**
Searles Dr. E6 5B **34**
Seaton Av. IG3: Ilf 4B **28**
Sebastian Av. CM15: Shenf 2A **6**
Sebastian Ct. IG11: Bark 1F **35**
Sebert Rd. E7 3A **26**

56 A-Z Romford

Second Av.—Strathfield Gdns.

Second Av. E12 . . . . .3C **26**
RM6: Chad H 3E **21**
RM10: Dag 1F **37**
Sedgefield Cl. RM3: Rom 1D **14**
Sedgefield Cres. RM3: Rom 2D **14**
Sedgemoor Dr. RM10: Dag 3A **30**
Seedbed Cen., The
RM7: Rom 5E **23**
Selborne Av. E12 . . . . .3E **27**
Selborne Rd. IG1: Ilf 1E **27**
Selinas La. RM8: Dag 5G **21**
Selsdon Cl. RM5: Col R 5C **12**
Selwood Rd. CM14: Bwood 6B **4**
Selwyn Av. IG3: Ilf 4B **20**
Seton Gdns. RM9: Dag 6E **29**
Settle Rd. RM3: Rom 1E **15**
Seven Arches Rd.
CM14: Bwood 6F **5**
SEVEN KINGS **6A 20**
Seven Kings Rd. IG3: Ilf 6A **20**
Seven Kings Station (Rail) **6A 20**
Sevenoaks Cl. RM3: Rom 1A **14**
Seventh Av. E12 . . . . .3D **26**
Severn Av. RM2: Rom 1H **23**
Severn Dr. RM14: Upm 4H **25**
Sexton Cl. RM13: Rain 1B **38**
Seymer Rd. RM1: Rom 1D **22**
Seymour Gdns. IG1: Ilf 6D **18**
Seymour Pl. RM11: Horn 5B **24**
Shafter Rd. RM10: Dag 5C **30**
Shaftesbury Ct. *E6 . . . . .6A 34*
(off Sapphire Cl.)
Shaftesbury Rd. E7 . . . . .6A **26**
RM1: Rom 4F **23**
Shaftesburys, The IG11: Bark . . .2C **34**
Shakespeare Cres. E12 . . . . .5D **26**
Shakespeare Rd. RM1: Rom 4F **23**
Shakespeare Sq. IG6: Ilf 3G **9**
Shaw Av. IG11: Bark 2C **36**
Shaw Cl. RM11: Horn 6H **23**
Shaw Cres. CM13: Hut 1D **6**
Shaw Gdns. IG11: Bark 2C **36**
Shearwater Cl. IG11: Bark 3G **35**
Sheepcotes Rd. RM6: Chad H . . .2G **21**
Sheffield Dr. RM3: Rom 2E **15**
Sheffield Gdns. RM3: Rom 2E **15**
Sheila Cl. RM5: Col R 4B **12**
Sheila Rd. RM5: Col R 4B **12**
Sheilings, The RM11: Horn 3D **24**
Sheldon Av. IG5: Ilf 6F **9**
Sheldon Rd. RM9: Dag 6G **29**
Shelley Av. E12 . . . . .5C **26**
RM12: Horn 1F **31**
Shelley Rd. CM13: Hut 3D **6**
SHENFIELD **2A 6**
Shenfield Cres. CM15: Bwood 5G **5**
Shenfield Gdns. CM13: Hut 2B **6**
Shenfield Grn. CM15: Shenf 3A **6**
Shenfield Pl. CM15: Shenf 3G **5**
Shenfield Rd.
CM15: Bwood, Shenf 5F **5**
Shenfield Station (Rail) **3A 6**
Shen Pl. Almshouses
CM15: Bwood 5F **5**
Shenstone Gdns. RM3: Rom 5A **14**
Shepherds Cl. RM6: Chad H 3F **21**
Shepherds Hill RM3: Hrld W 6E **15**
Shepherd's Path
CM14: S Weald 3A **4**
Sheppey Gdns. RM9: Dag 6E **29**
Sheppey Rd. RM9: Dag 6D **28**
Sherborne Gdns. RM5: Col R . . .2A **12**
Shere Rd. IG2: Ilf 3E **19**
Sheridan Cl. RM3: Rom 4A **14**
Sheridan Rd. E12 . . . . .4C **26**
Sheringham Av. E12 . . . . .3D **26**
RM7: Rom 4C **22**
Sheringham Dr. IG11: Bark 4B **28**
Sherman Gdns. RM6: Chad H . . .4E **21**
Sherrard Rd. E7 . . . . .5A **26**
E12 .5A **26**
Sherry M. IG11: Bark 6H **27**
Sherwood Av. E18 . . . . .1A **18**
Sherwood Gdns. IG11: Bark 6H **27**
Sherwood Rd. IG6: Ilf 2H **19**
Shevon Way CM14: Bwood 1B **16**
Shillibeer Wlk. IG7: Chig 1B **10**
Shipton Cl. RM8: Dag 2F **29**
Shirley Gdns. IG11: Bark 5A **28**
RM12: Horn 1A **32**
Shoebury Rd. E6 . . . . .6D **26**
Shortcrofts Rd. RM9: Dag 5H **29**
Shorter Av. CM15: Shenf 3H **5**
Showcase Cinema
Barking 3D 34
Shrewsbury Rd. E7 . . . . .4B **26**
Shrubberies, The IG7: Chig 2G **9**
Shrubbery, The RM14: Upm 2G **33**
Shrublands Cl. IG7: Chig 3G **9**
Sibley Gro. E12 . . . . .6C **26**
Sickle Cnr. RM9: Dag 4F **37**
Sidney Elson Way E6 . . . . .2A **34**
Sierra Dr. RM9: Dag 2F **37**
Silver Birches CM13: Hut 4A **6**
Silver Birch M. IG6: Ilf 3G **9**
Silverdale Av. IG3: Ilf 3A **20**
Silverdale Dr. RM12: Horn 4H **31**
Silvermere Av. RM5: Col R 3B **12**
Silver Way RM7: Mawney 1B **22**
Simpson Rd. RM13: Rain 5F **31**
Sims Cl. RM1: Rom 2F **23**
Singleton Cl. RM12: Horn 3F **31**
Singleton Rd. RM9: Dag 4H **29**
Sippets Ct. IG1: Ilf 6H **19**
Sir Francis Way
CM14: Bwood 5D **4**
Sisley Rd. IG11: Bark 1E **35**
Siviter Way RM10: Dag 6B **30**
Sixpenny Ct. IG11: Bark 5G **27**
Sixth Av. E12 . . . . .3D **26**
Skeffington Rd.
E6 . . . . .6D **26** & 6D **26**
Skipper Ct. IG11: Bark 1C **34**
Skipsey Av. E6 . . . . .3A **34**
Slaney Rd. RM1: Rom 3E **23**
Slewins Cl. RM11: Horn 3A **24**
Slewins La. RM11: Horn 3A **24**
Smart Cl. RM3: Rom 5H **13**
Smeaton Rd. IG8: Wfd G 2D **8**
Snakes La. E.
IG8: Buck H, Wfd G 3A **8**
Snakes La. W. IG8: Wfd G 3A **8**
Snowdon Ct. RM2: Rom 2A **24**
Snowdrop Path RM3: Rom 4B **14**
Snowshill Rd. E12 . . . . .4C **26**
Solar Ho. E6 . . . . .5A **34**
Somerby Rd. IG11: Bark 6H **27**
Somersby Gdns. IG4: Ilf 3D **18**
Somerset Gdns. RM11: Horn 6E **25**
Somerville Rd. RM6: Chad H . . .4E **21**
Sorrel Wlk. RM1: Rom 1F **23**
Southall Ho. *RM3: Rom 3C 14*
(off Kingsbridge Cir.)
Southall Way CM14: Bwood 1B **16**
South Block RM2: Horn 1B **24**
Sth. Boundary Rd. E12 . . . . .2D **26**
Southbourne Gdns. IG1: Ilf 4G **27**
Southbury Cl. RM12: Horn 4B **32**
Southchurch Rd. E6 . . . . .2A **34**
South Cl. RM10: Dag 1E **37**
Sth. Cross Rd. IG6: Ilf 3G **19**
Southdale IG7: Chig 3H **9**
Southdown Cres. IG2: Ilf 3A **20**
Southdown Rd. RM11: Horn 5H **23**
South Dr. CM14: War 1F **17**
E12 .2C **26**
RM2: Rom 1A **24**
Southend Arterial Rd.
RM2: Hrld W 6B **14**
RM3: Hrld W 6B **14**
RM11: Horn, Upm 6B **14**
RM14: Gt War, Upm 1C **24**
South End Rd. RM12: Horn 5H **31**
RM13: Horn, Rain 2C **38**
Southend Rd. E6 . . . . .6D **26**
IG8: Wfd G 6A **8**
Southern Way RM7: Rom 4A **22**
Sth. Esk Rd. E7 . . . . .5A **26**
South Essex Crematorium
RM14: Upm 4H **33**
South Ga. Rd. E12 . . . . .2B **26**
Sth. Hall Dr. RM13: Rain 5D **38**
SOUTH HORNCHURCH **2B 38**
South Pk. Cres. IG1: Ilf 2H **27**
South Pk. Dr. IG3: Ilf 1A **28**
IG11: Bark 4A **28**
South Pk. Rd. IG1: Ilf 2H **27**
South Pk. Ter. IG1: Ilf 2A **28**
South Pk. Vs. IG3: Ilf 3A **28**
South Rd. RM6: Chad H 3E **21**
(Chadwell Heath La.)
RM6: Chad H 4G **21**
(West Rd.)
Southsea Ho. *RM3: Rom 2B 14*
(off Darlington Gdns.)
South St. CM14: Bwood 5E **5**
RM1: Rom 3E **23**
(not continuous)
RM13: Rain 2G **37**
Southview Cres. IG2: Ilf 4F **19**
South Vw. Dr. E18 . . . . .1A **18**
RM14: Upm 2E **33**
Southview Pde. RM13: Rain 3H **37**
Southways Pde. IG2: Ilf 3E **19**
SOUTH WEALD **5A 4**
Sth. Weald Rd. CM14: Bwood 6C **4**
Southwold Dr. IG11: Bark 4C **28**
Sth. Woodford to Barking Relief Rd.
E11 .1A **18**
E12 .3E **27**
IG1: Ilf 1A **18**
IG4: Ilf 1A **18**
Southwood Gdns. IG2: Ilf 2F **19**
Sovereign Rd. IG11: Bark 3A **36**
Sowrey Av. RM13: Rain 5F **31**
Spalt Cl. CM13: Hut 5B **6**
Sparks Cl. RM8: Dag 1F **29**
Sparrow Grn. RM10: Dag 2B **30**
Sparsholt Cl. *IG11: Bark 1E 35*
(off St John's Rd.)
Sparsholt Rd. IG11: Bark 1E **35**
Spearpoint Gdns. IG2: Ilf 3B **20**
Spectrum Twr. *IG1: Ilf 1G 27*
(off Hainault St.)
Spencer Cl. IG8: Wfd G 2A **8**
Spencer Rd. IG3: Ilf 6B **20**
RM13: Rain 3H **37**
Spenser Cres. RM14: Upm 5G **25**
Spey Way RM1: Rom 4E **13**
Spilsby Rd. RM3: Rom 4B **14**
Spingate Cl. RM12: Horn 4A **32**
Spinnaker Cl. IG11: Bark 3H **35**
Spinney, The CM13: Hut 2C **6**
Spinney Cl. RM13: Rain 2A **38**
Spinney Gdns. RM9: Dag 4G **29**
Spires, The CM14: Bwood 5F **5**
Spital La. CM14: Bwood 6B **4**
Springbank Av. RM12: Horn 4A **32**
Spring Cl. RM8: Dag 6F **21**
Springfarm Cl. RM13: Rain 3F **39**
Springfield Av. CM13: Hut 3E **7**
Springfield Ct. IG1: Ilf 4F **27**
RM14: Upm 2G **33**
Springfield Dr. IG2: Ilf 3G **19**
Springfield Gdns. IG8: Wfd G 4A **8**
RM14: Upm 2F **33**
Springfield Rd. E6 . . . . .6D **26**
Spring Gdns. IG8: Wfd G 4A **8**
RM7: Rom 3C **22**
RM12: Horn 3H **31**
Spring Gdns. Bus. Pk.
RM7: Rom 3C **22**
Spring Health Leisure Club
Brentwood 4E 17
Springpond Rd. RM9: Dag 4G **29**
Springwood Way RM1: Rom 3G **23**
Spurgate CM13: Hut 5A **6**
Spurling Rd. RM9: Dag 5H **29**
Spurway Pde. *IG2: Ilf 3D 18*
(off Woodford Av.)
Squadrons App. RM12: Horn 5A **32**
Square, The CM14: Bwood 5E **5**
IG1: Ilf 5E **19**
Squires, The RM7: Rom 4C **22**
SQUIRREL'S HEATH **1B 24**
Squirrels Heath Av.
RM2: Rom 1H **23**
Squirrels Heath La.
RM2: Horn, Rom 2A **24**
RM11: Horn, Rom 2A **24**
Squirrels Heath Rd.
RM3: Hrld W 1C **24**
Squirrel's La. IG9: Buck H 1B **8**
Stafford Av. RM11: Horn 1B **24**
Stafford Ind. Est. RM11: Horn . . .1B **24**
Stafford Rd. E7 . . . . .6A **26**
Staggart Grn. IG7: Chig, Ilf 2B **10**
Staines Rd. IG1: Ilf 4G **27**
Stainforth Rd. IG2: Ilf 5H **19**
Stalham Way IG6: Ilf 5F **9**
Stamford Gdns. RM9: Dag 6E **29**
Stamford Rd. RM9: Dag 1H **35**
Standen Av. RM12: Horn 2C **32**
Standfield Gdns. RM10: Dag 5A **30**
Standfield Rd. RM10: Dag 4A **30**
Stanford Cl. IG8: Wfd G 2C **8**
RM7: Rom 4B **22**
Stanford Ho. IG11: Bark 2H **35**
Stanhope Gdns. IG1: Ilf 6D **18**
RM8: Dag 2H **29**
Stanhope Rd. RM8: Dag 1H **29**
RM13: Rain 2C **38**
Stanley Av. IG11: Bark 2F **35**
RM2: Rom 2G **23**
RM8: Dag 6H **21**
Stanley Cl. RM2: Rom 2G **23**
RM12: Horn 1A **32**
Stanley Rd. E12 . . . . .4C **26**
IG1: Ilf 1H **27**
RM12: Horn 1A **32**
Stanley Rd. Nth. RM13: Rain . . .1A **38**
Stanley Rd. Sth. RM13: Rain . . .2B **38**
Stansgate Rd. RM10: Dag 1A **30**
Stansted Cl. RM12: Horn 5H **31**
Stanway Cl. IG7: Chig 2A **10**
Stanwyck Dr. IG7: Chig 2G **9**
Stanwyck Gdns. RM3: Rom 2H **13**
Stapleford Av. IG2: Ilf 3A **20**
Stapleford Gdns. RM5: Col R . . .3A **12**
Stapleford Way IG11: Bark 3H **35**
Staples Ho. *E6 . . . . .6A 34*
(off Savage Gdns.)
Stapleton Cres. RM13: Rain 5G **31**
Star Bus. Cen. RM13: Rain 5H **37**
Starch Ho. La. IG6: Ilf 6H **9**
Starmans Cl. RM9: Dag 1C **36**
Station App. IG8: Wfd G 3A **8**
IG9: Buck H 1B **8**
RM14: Upm 1G **33**
Station Chambers *E6 . . . . .6C 26*
(off High St. Nth.)
Station La. RM12: Horn 2B **32**
Station Pde. E6 . . . . .6C **26**
IG9: Buck H 1B **8**
IG11: Bark 6G **27**
RM1: Rom 4E **23**
RM9: Dag 5A **30**
RM12: Horn 3H **31**
Station Rd. E12 . . . . .3C **26**
IG1: Ilf 2F **27**
IG6: Ilf 1H **19**
IG7: Chig 1F **9**
RM2: Rom 2H **23**
RM3: Hrld W 5D **14**
RM6: Chad H, Dag 5F **21**
RM14: Upm 1G **33**
Station Sq. RM2: Rom 2H **23**
Station Wlk. *IG1: Ilf 1F 27*
(in Exchange, The)
Station Way IG9: Buck H 1A **8**
Staverton Rd. RM11: Horn 4B **24**
Steadman Ho. *RM10: Dag 2A 30*
(off Uvedale Rd.)
Stebbing Way IG11: Bark 2G **35**
Steed Cl. RM11: Horn 1H **31**
Stephen Av. RM13: Rain 5G **31**
Stephens Cl. RM3: Rom 2A **14**
Ster Century Cinemas 4E 23
Sterling Ind. Est. RM10: Dag . . .3B **30**
Stern Cl. IG11: Bark 2A **36**
Sterry Cres. RM10: Dag 4A **30**
Sterry Gdns. RM10: Dag 5A **30**
Sterry Rd. IG11: Bark 1F **35**
RM10: Dag 3A **30**
Stevenage Rd. E6 . . . . .5E **27**
Stevens Rd. RM8: Dag 2D **28**
Stevens Way IG7: Chig 1A **10**
Stewards Wlk. RM1: Rom 3E **23**
Stewart Av. RM14: Upm 2F **33**
Stewart Rainbird Ho.
E12 .4E 27
(off Parkhurst Rd.)
Stirling Cl. RM13: Rain 3D **38**
Stockdale Rd. RM8: Dag 1H **29**
Stocker Gdns. RM9: Dag 6E **29**
Stockland Rd. RM7: Rom 4D **22**
Stoke Av. IG6: Ilf 3C **10**
Stoke Rd. RM13: Rain 2F **39**
Stokes Cotts. IG6: Ilf 5G **9**
Stonard Rd. RM8: Dag 4D **28**
Stone Cl. RM8: Dag 1H **29**
Stonehall Av. IG1: Ilf 4C **18**
Stoneleigh Ct. IG5: Ilf 1C **18**
Stoneleigh Rd. IG5: Ilf 1C **18**
Stonewall E6 . . . . .5A **34**
Stoneycroft Rd. IG8: Wfd G 3C **8**
Storr Gdns. CM13: Hut 1D **6**
Stour Rd. RM10: Dag 1A **30**
Stour Way RM14: Upm 2A **40**
Stradbroke Dr. IG7: Chig 3E **9**
Stradbroke Gro. IG5: Ilf 1C **18**
Stradbroke Pk. IG7: Chig 3F **9**
Strafford Av. IG5: Ilf 6E **9**
Straight Rd. RM3: Rom 2H **13**
Strait Rd. E6 . . . . .6A **34**
Stratford Cl. IG11: Bark 6C **28**
RM10: Dag 6C **30**
Stratford Ho. *RM3: Rom 3B 14*
(off Dartfields)
Strathfield Gdns. IG11: Bark 5H **27**

A-Z Romford 57

Strathmore Gdns.—Ulverston Ho.

Strathmore Gdns.
RM12: Horn 6F 23
Stratton Dr. IG11: Bark 4A 28
Stratton Rd. RM3: Rom 2E 15
Stratton Wlk. RM3: Rom 2E 15
Strone Rd. E7 5A 26
E12 5A 26
Strood Av. RM7: Rush G 6D 22
Stroud Ho. *RM3: Rom 2B 14*
(off Montgomery Cres.)
Stroud's Cl. RM6: Chad H 3D 20
Stuart Cl. CM15: Pil H 1D 4
Stuart Rd. IG11: Bark 6B 28
Stuarts *RM11: Horn 6D 24*
(off High St.)
Stubbers La. RM14: Upm 5H 33
Stubbs M. *RM8: Dag 3D 28*
(off Marlborough Rd.)
Studley Dr. IG4: Ilf 4B 18
Studley Rd. E7 5A 26
RM9: Dag 6F 29
Stukeley Rd. E7 6A 26
Sudbury E6 5A 34
Sudbury Rd. IG11: Bark 4B 28
Sudburys Farm Rd.
CM12: L Bur 6H 7
Suffolk Ct. IG3: Ilf 4A 20
Suffolk Rd. IG3: Ilf 4A 20
IG11: Bark 6H 27
RM10: Dag 4C 30
Suffolk Way RM11: Horn 2E 25
Sugden Way IG11: Bark 2F 35
Summerton Way SE28 6B 36
Summit Dr. IG8: Wfd G 6B 8
Sunderland Way E12 1B 26
Sunflower Way RM3: Hrld W 5B 14
Sungate Cotts. RM5: Col R 5H 11
Sunningdale Av. IG11: Bark 1D 34
RM13: Rain 4D 38
Sunningdale Cl. SE28 6C 36
Sunningdale Rd. RM13: Rain 6G 31
Sunnings La. RM14: Upm 4G 33
Sunnycroft Gdns. RM14: Upm 3B 40
Sunnydene Cl. RM3: Hrld W 4D 14
Sunnymede Dr. IG2: Ilf 3F 19
IG6: Ilf 3F 19
Sunny M. RM5: Col R 4C 12
Sunnyside Gdns. RM14: Upm 2G 33
Sunnyside Rd. IG1: Ilf 2G 27
Sun Ray Av. CM13: Hut 2E 7
Sunrise Av. RM12: Horn 2A 32
Sunset Ct. IG8: Wfd G 4A 8
Sunset Dr. RM4: Have B 2H 13
Surlingham Cl. SE28 6B 36
Surman Cres. CM13: Hut 3C 6
Surmans Cl. RM9: Dag 1A 36
Surrey Dr. RM11: Horn 2E 25
Surrey Rd. IG11: Bark 6A 28
RM10: Dag 4B 30
Surridge Cl. RM13: Rain 3E 39
Susan Cl. RM7: Mawney 1C 22
Susan Lawrence Ho. *E12 3E 27*
(off Walton Rd.)
Sussex Av. RM3: Hrld W 4D 14
Sussex Cl. IG4: Ilf 3D 18
Sussex Rd. CM14: War 1D 16
E6 1A 34
Sutherland Ho. IG8: Wfd G 4E 9
Sutton Gdns. IG11: Bark 1E 35
Sutton Grn. *IG11: Bark 1E 35*
(off Felton Gdns.)
Sutton Rd. IG11: Bark 2E 35
Suttons Av. RM12: Horn 2A 32
Suttons Bus. Pk. RM13: Rain 3H 37
Suttons Gdns. RM12: Horn 2B 32
Suttons La. RM12: Horn 4B 32
Swallow Ct. IG2: Ilf 3F 19
Swallow Wlk. RM12: Horn 5H 31
Swan Av. RM14: Upm 4B 40
Swanbourne Dr. RM12: Horn 4A 32
Swan M. RM7: Mawney 2B 22
Swan Paddock CM14: Bwood 5E 5
Swan Wlk. RM1: Rom 3E 23
Sweetland Ct. RM8: Dag 5D 28
Swift Cl. RM14: Upm 4A 40
SE28 6H 35
Swindon Cl. IG3: Ilf 1A 28
RM3: Rom 2D 14
Swindon Gdns. RM3: Rom 2D 14
Swindon La. RM3: Rom 2D 14
Sycamore Av. RM14: Upm 2E 33
Sycamore Ct. RM12: Horn 6F 23
Sycamore Dr. CM14: Bwood 4E 5
Sycamore Gro. RM2: Rom 6G 13
Sycamore Wlk. IG6: Ilf 2G 19
Sydenham Cl. RM1: Rom 1F 23
Sydney Rd. IG6: Ilf 6G 9
Sydney Russell Leisure Cen. 4G 29
Sylvan Av. RM6: Chad H 4H 21
RM11: Horn 4C 24
Sylvan Rd. IG1: Ilf 1G 27
Sylvan Way RM8: Dag 3D 28
Sylvester Gdns. IG6: Ilf 2D 10
Sylvia Av. CM13: Hut 5C 6
Sylvia Pankhurst Ho.
RM10: Dag 2A 30
(off Wythenshawe Rd.)
Syracuse Av. RM13: Rain 3G 39

T

Tabors Ct. CM15: Shenf 3A 6
Tabrums Way RM14: Upm 3A 40
Tadlows Cl. RM14: Upm 4F 33
Tadworth Pde. RM12: Horn 3H 31
Takeley Cl. RM5: Col R 6D 12
Talbot Gdns. IG3: Ilf 1C 28
Talbot Rd. E6 2A 34
RM9: Dag 5H 29
Talbrook CM14: Bwood 6B 4
Talgarth Ho. *RM3: Rom 3C 14*
(off Kingsbridge Cir.)
Talisman Cl. IG3: Ilf 6D 20
Tallis Way CM14: Gt War 2D 16
Tallon Rd. CM13: Hut 1E 7
Tall Trees Cl. RM11: Horn 4B 24
Tally-Ho Dr. CM13: Hut 4H 7
Tamar Cl. RM14: Upm 2A 40
Tamar Sq. IG8: Wfd G 3A 8
Tangent Link RM3: Rom 5B 14
Tangmere Cres. RM12: Horn 5H 31
Tanners La. IG6: Ilf 1G 19
Tanner St. IG11: Bark 5G 27
Tannery Cl. RM10: Dag 2B 30
Tansy Cl. E6 6A 34
RM3: Rom 3C 14
Tantony Gro. RM6: Chad H 1F 21
Tarnworth Rd. RM3: Rom 2E 15
Tasker Ho. IG11: Bark 2D 34
Taunton Cl. IG6: Ilf 3B 10
Taunton Ho. *RM3: Rom 2D 14*
(off Redcar Rd.)
Taunton Rd. RM3: Rom 1A 14
Tavistock Cl. RM3: Rom 5B 14
Tavistock Gdns. IG3: Ilf 3A 28
Tavistock Ho. IG8: Wfd G 3E 9
Tawny Av. RM14: Upm 4F 33
Taylor Cl. RM5: Col R 4A 12
Tay Way RM1: Rom 5F 13
Ted Hennem Ho. RM10: Dag 2B 30
Tees Cl. RM14: Upm 4H 25
Tees Dr. RM3: Rom 1B 14
Telegraph M. IG3: Ilf 6C 20
Telham Rd. E6 2A 34
Tempest Way RM13: Rain 5G 31
Templar Dr. SE28 6B 36
Templar Ho. RM13: Rain 2H 37
Temple Av. RM8: Dag 6A 22
Temple Gdns. RM8: Dag 2F 29
Temple Rd. E6 6C 26
Tenbury Cl. E7 4B 26
Tenby Cl. RM6: Chad H 4G 21
Tenby Rd. RM6: Chad H 4G 21
Tendring Ct. CM13: Hut 1D 6
Tendring Way RM6: Chad H 3E 21
Tennyson Av. E12 6C 26
Tennyson Rd. CM13: Hut 3C 6
RM3: Rom 4A 14
Tennyson Way RM12: Horn 1F 31
Tenterden Rd. RM8: Dag 1H 29
Tercel Path IG7: Chig 1D 10
Terling Rd. RM8: Dag 1A 30
Terlings, The CM14: Bwood 6C 4
Tern Gdns. RM14: Upm 4A 40
Tern Way CM14: Bwood 1A 16
Terrace Wlk. RM9: Dag 4G 29
Thackeray Dr. RM6: Chad H 5C 20
Thal Massing Cl. CM13: Hut 5B 6
Thames Av. RM9: Dag, Rain 4F 37
Thamesbank Pl. SE28 6A 36
Thames Cl. RM13: Rain 6D 38
Thames Gateway RM9: Dag 2D 36
RM13: Avel, Rain, Wenn 5A 38
Thames Gateway Pk.
RM9: Dag 3D 36
Thameshill Av. RM5: Col R 6C 12
Thameside Community Nature
Reserve 4G 35
Thameside Leisure Cen. 6G 35
Thameside Pk. City Farm 3G 35
Thameside Wlk. SE28 6G 35
THAMESMEAD NORTH 6B 36
Thames Rd. IG11: Bark 3F 35
Thatches Gro. RM6: Chad H 2G 21
Thaxted Bold CM13: Hut 1D 6
Thaxted Grn. CM13: Hut 1C 6
Thaxted Ho. RM10: Dag 6B 30
Thaxted Wlk. RM13: Rain 6E 31
Thetford Gdns. RM9: Dag 6G 29
Thetford Rd. RM9: Dag 6F 29
Theydon Bold CM13: Hut 1E 7
Theydon Gdns. RM13: Rain 6E 31
Theydon Gro. IG8: Wfd G 3A 8
Thicket Gro. RM9: Dag 5E 29
Third Av. E12 3C 26
RM6: Chad H 4E 21
RM10: Dag 1F 37
Thistledene Av. RM5: Col R 2B 12
Thomas Cl. CM15: Bwood 5G 5
Thomas Cribb M. E6 6A 34
Thomas England Ho.
RM7: Rom 4D 22
(off Waterloo Gdns.)
Thomas Sims Ct. RM12: Rain 5H 31
Thompson Cl. IG1: Ilf 1G 27
Thompson Rd. RM9: Dag 2H 29
Thornbury Ho. *RM3: Rom 2B 14*
(off Bridgwater Wlk.)
Thorncroft RM11: Horn 4H 23
Thorndales CM14: War 1F 17
Thorndene SE28 6H 35
Thorndon Country Pk. 3H 17
Thorngrove Rd. E13 6A 26
Thornhill Gdns. IG11: Bark 6A 28
Thorn La. RM13: Rain 2F 39
Thornridge CM14: Bwood 4D 4
Thornton Rd. IG1: Ilf 3F 27
Thornton's Farm Av.
RM7: Rush G 6C 22
Thornwood Cl. E18 6A 8
Thorogood Way RM13: Rain 1A 38
Thorold Rd. IG1: Ilf 1F 27
Thorpe Bold CM13: Hut 1E 7
Thorpedale Gdns. IG2: Ilf 2E 19
IG6: Ilf 2F 19
Thorpe Lodge RM11: Horn 4C 24
Thorpe Rd. IG11: Bark 6H 27
Thorrington Bold CM13: Hut 1D 6
Thrapston Ho. *RM3: Rom 2C 14*
(off Dagnam Pk. Dr.)
Thrift Grn. CM13: Bwood 6A 6
Thurlby Cl. IG8: Wfd G 2D 8
Thurlestone Av. IG3: Bark, Ilf 3B 28
Thurloe Gdns. RM1: Rom 4F 23
Thurlow Gdns. IG6: Ilf 3H 9
Thurso Cl. RM3: Hrld W 3F 15
Tilbury Rd. E6 2A 34
Tillingham Bold CM13: Hut 1D 6
Tillotson Rd. IG1: Ilf 5E 19
Tilney Rd. RM9: Dag 5H 29
(not continuous)
Timberdene Av. IG6: Ilf 5G 9
Tindall Cl. RM3: Hrld W 6D 14
Tindall M. RM12: Horn 2A 32
Tine Rd. IG7: Chig 2A 10
(not continuous)
Tintagel Ct. RM11: Horn 6E 25
Tippett Ct. E6 2A 34
Tiptree Cl. RM11: Horn 6E 25
Tiptree Ct. CM13: Hut 1D 6
Tiptree Cres. IG5: Ilf 6E 9
Tiverton Av. IG5: Ilf 1E 19
Tiverton Gro. RM3: Rom 2E 15
Todd Cl. RM13: Rain 4F 39
Tolbut Ct. RM1: Rom 4F 23
Tollesbury Ct. CM13: Hut 1D 6
Tollesbury Gdns. IG6: Ilf 1H 19
Tollgate Rd. E6 5A 34
Tolworth Gdns. RM6: Chad H 3F 21
Tolworth Pde. RM6: Chad H 3G 21
Tomkyns La.
RM14: Upm 6H 15 & 1A 40
Tomlins Orchard IG11: Bark 1C 34
Tomlyns Cl. CM13: Hut 2E 7
Tom Mann Cl. IG11: Bark 1E 35
Tomswood Ct. IG6: Ilf 5G 9
Tomswood Hill IG6: Ilf 3F 9
Tomswood Rd. IG7: Chig 3E 9
Tonbridge Rd. RM3: Rom 4B 14
Torbitt Way IG2: Ilf 3B 20
Toronto Av. E12 3D 26
Toronto Rd. IG1: Ilf 6F 19
Torquay Gdns. IG4: Ilf 2B 18
Torrance Cl. RM11: Horn 6H 23
Torrington Rd. RM8: Dag 6H 21
Tourist Info. Cen.
Brentwood 5F 5
Ilford 2F 27
Tower Cl. IG6: Ilf 3F 9
Tower Ct. CM14: Bwood 5E 5
Tower Hill CM14: Bwood 5E 5
Town Quay IG11: Bark 1B 34
Town Quay Wharf IG11: Bark 1B 34
Trader Rd. E6 6B 34
Trafalgar Bus. Cen. IG11: Bark 4F 35
Trafalgar Rd. RM13: Rain 2B 38
Trafford Cl. IG6: Ilf 3B 10
Tree Top M. RM10: Dag 5D 30
Tree Tops CM15: Bwood 4E 5
Trefgarne Rd. RM10: Dag 1A 30
Trehearn Rd. IG6: Ilf 4H 9
Trelawney Rd. IG6: Ilf 4H 9
Trenance Gdns. IG3: Ilf 2C 28
Trent Av. RM14: Upm 4H 25
Trentbridge Cl. IG6: Ilf 3B 10
Tresco Gdns. IG3: Ilf 1C 28
RM5: Col R 2C 12
Tresham Rd. IG11: Bark 6B 28
Treswell Rd. RM9: Dag 1C 36
Trevelyan Av. E12 3D 26
Triangle, The IG11: Bark 5G 27
Trillo Ct. IG2: Ilf 5A 20
Tring Cl. IG2: Ilf 3H 19
RM3: Rom 1D 14
Tring Gdns. RM3: Rom 1C 14
Tring Wlk. RM3: Rom 1C 14
Trinidad Gdns. RM10: Dag 6D 30
Trinity Rd. IG6: Ilf 1G 19
Triumph Ho. IG11: Bark 3G 35
Triumph Rd. E6 6A 34
Troon Cl. SE28 6B 36
Troopers Dr. RM3: Rom 1B 14
Trot Wood IG7: Chig 3H 9
Trotwood Cl. CM15: Shenf 4G 5
Trowbridge Rd. RM3: Rom 3B 14
Truesdale Rd. E6 6A 34
Truro Gdns. IG1: Ilf 5C 18
Truro Wlk. RM3: Rom 3A 14
Truston's Gdns. RM11: Horn 5G 23
Tryfan Cl. IG4: Ilf 3B 18
Tuck Rd. RM13: Rain 5G 31
Tudor Av. RM2: Rom 1G 23
Tudor Cl. CM15: Shenf 2A 6
IG7: Chig 1E 9
IG8: Wfd G 2A 8
Tudor Ct. RM3: Hrld W 3F 15
Tudor Cres. IG6: Ilf 3F 9
Tudor Dr. RM2: Rom 2G 23
Tudor Gdns. RM2: Rom 2G 23
RM14: Upm 1G 33
Tudor M. RM1: Rom 3F 23
Tudor Pde. RM6: Chad H 5F 21
Tudor Rd. IG11: Bark 1F 35
Tufter Rd. IG7: Chig 2B 10
Tulip Cl. CM15: Pil H 1D 4
RM3: Rom 3A 14
Tulip Gdns. IG1: Ilf 5F 27
Tunnan Leys E6 6A 34
Tunstall Av. IG6: Ilf 3C 10
Turnage Rd. RM8: Dag 6G 21
Turnbury Cl. SE28 6B 36
Turner Rd. RM12: Horn 1F 31
Turpin Av. RM5: Col R 3A 12
Turpin's La. IG8: Wfd G 2D 8
Tweed Glen RM1: Rom 4D 12
Tweed Grn. RM1: Rom 4D 12
Tweed Way RM1: Rom 4D 12
Twine Cl. IG11: Bark 3H 35
Twyford Rd. IG1: Ilf 4G 27
Tyburns, The CM13: Hut 5C 6
Tyle Grn. RM11: Horn 2C 24
Tylehurst Gdns. IG1: Ilf 4G 27
Tylers Cres. RM12: Horn 4A 32
Tyler Way CM14: Bwood 4D 4
Tylney Rd. E7 3A 26
Tyne Cl. RM14: Upm 4H 25
Tynemouth Cl. E6 6B 34
Tyrell Pl. CM15: Shenf 4H 5
Tyrell Ri. CM14: War 2E 17
Tyrells Cl. RM14: Upm 1F 33
Tyrone Rd. E6 2A 34

U

Udall Gdns. RM5: Col R 3A 12
Ullswater Way RM12: Horn 4G 31
Ulverston Ho. *RM3: Rom 3C 14*
(off Kingsbridge Cir.)

Underwood Rd. IG8: Wfd G 4A 8
Unity Trad. Est. IG8: Wfd G ...6B 8
University of East London
  Barking Campus 3C 28
Uphall Rd. IG1: Ilf 4F 27
Uphavering Ho. RM12: Horn ...1A 32
Upland Ct. Rd. RM3: Hrld W ...6D 14
Uplands End IG8: Wfd G 4C 8
Uplands Rd. CM14: War 2G 17
  IG8: Wfd G 4C 8
  RM6: Chad H 1F 21
UPMINSTER 1G 33
Upminster Bridge Station (Tube)
  ....1E 33
Upminster Rd. RM11: Horn ...1D 32
  RM12: Horn 1D 32
  IG12: Ilf 1D 32
  RM14: Upm 1D 32
Upminster Rd. Nth.
  RM13: Rain 3E 39
Upminster Rd. Sth.
  RM13: Rain 4C 38
Upminster Smock Mill 1F 33
Upminster Station (Rail & Tube)
  ....1G 33
Upminster Tithe Barn &
  Agricultural Folk Mus. ...5H 25
Upney Ct. RM12: Horn 4B 32
Upney La. IG11: Bark 5A 28
Upney Station (Tube) 6B 28
Uppark Dr. IG2: Ilf 4G 19
Up. Brentwood Rd.
  RM2: Rom 2A 24
Upper Cornsland CM14: Bwood ...3D 17
Up. Rainham Rd. RM12: Horn ...6F 23
Upper Ryle CM14: Bwood 3D 4
Upton Ho. *RM3: Rom* *2B 14*
  (off Barnstaple Rd.)
Upton Pk. Rd. E7 ....6A 26
Upward Ct. RM1: Rom 2F 23
Urban Av. RM7: Rom 2A 32
Urswick Gdns. RM9: Dag 6G 29
Urswick Rd. RM9: Dag 6F 29
Uvedale Rd. RM10: Dag 2A 30

V

Vale, The CM14: Bwood 4E 5
Vale Cl. CM15: Pil H 1B 4
Valence Av. RM8: Dag 6F 21
Valence Cir. RM8: Dag 2F 29
Valence House Mus. & Gallery
  ....2G 29
Valence Wood Rd. RM8: Dag ...2F 29
Valentines Rd. IG1: Ilf 6F 19
Valentine's Way
  RM7: Rush G 1E 31
Valiant Cl. RM7: Mawney ...6B 12
Vanguard Cl. RM7: Mawney ...6A 12
Vaughan Av. RM12: Horn 3B 32
Vaughan Gdns. IG1: Ilf 5D 18
Vaughan Williams Way
  CM14: Gt War, War 3C 16
Venables Cl. RM10: Dag 3B 30
Venette Cl. RM13: Rain 5D 38
Ventnor Gdns. IG11: Bark ...5A 28
Veny Cres. RM12: Horn 4B 32
Verderers Rd. IG7: Chig ...2C 10
Verney Gdns. RM9: Dag 3G 29
Verney Rd. RM9: Dag 3G 29
  (not continuous)
Vernon Av. E12 ....3D 26
Vernon Cres. CM13: Bwood ...6A 6
Vernon Rd. IG3: Ilf 6B 20
  RM5: Col R 2C 12
Veronica Cl. RM3: Rom 4A 14
Veronique Gdns. IG6: Ilf ...3G 19
Veysey Gdns. RM10: Dag 2A 30
Vicarage Cl. CM14: Bwood ...1A 16
Vicarage Cl. IG1: Ilf 4F 27
Vicarage Dr. IG11: Bark ...6G 27
Vicarage Fld. Shop. Cen.
  IG11: Bark 6G 27
Vicarage La. E6 ....3A 34
  IG1: Ilf 6H 19
  IG7: Chig 1A 10
Vicarage Rd. IG8: Wfd G 4C 8
  RM10: Dag 6B 30
  RM12: Horn 6G 23
Vicars Wlk. RM8: Dag 2D 28
Victor App. RM12: Horn 6B 24
Victor Cl. RM12: Horn 6B 24
Victor Ct. *RM12: Horn* *6B 24*
  (off Victor Wlk.)
Victor Gdns. RM12: Horn ...6B 24

Victoria Av. E6 ....6B 26
  RM5: Col R 3B 12
Victoria Ct. CM14: War 1E 17
  RM1: Rom 3G 23
Victoria Ho. E6 ....6A 34
  RM1: Rom 2A 24
Victoria Rd. CM14: War 1E 17
  E18 ....1A 18
  IG11: Bark 5F 27
  RM1: Rom 4F 23
  RM10: Dag 4B 30
Victor's Cres. CM13: Hut ...5B 6
Victor Wlk. RM12: Horn 6B 24
Victory Bus. Cen.
  RM7: Rush G 5C 22
Victory Rd. RM7: Rush G 5A 22
Victory Way RM7: Mawney ...6B 12
Vienna Cl. IG5: Ilf 6B 8
View Cl. IG7: Chig 2H 9
Vignoles Rd. RM7: Rush G ...5A 22
Viking Bus. Cen.
  RM7: Rush G 5C 22
Viking Way CM15: Pil H 2D 4
  RM13: Rain 4C 38
Village Way IG8: Ilf 2G 19
Vincent Cl. IG6: Ilf 3G 9
Vincent Rd. RM9: Dag 6G 29
  RM13: Rain 4E 39
Vine Cl. IG1: Ilf 4G 27
Vineries Cl. RM9: Dag 5H 29
Vine St. RM7: Rom 2C 22
Vine Way CM14: Bwood 4E 5
Virginia Cl. RM5: Col R ...4C 12
Virginia Gdns. IG6: Ilf ...6G 9
Vista Dr. IG4: Ilf 3B 18
Voyagers Cl. SE28 ....6A 36
Vulcan Cl. E6 ....6A 34

W

Wadeville Av. RM6: Chad H ...4G 21
Wagstaff Gdns. RM9: Dag ...6E 29
Wainfleet Rd. RM5: Col R ...6C 12
Wainwright Av. CM13: Hut ...2D 6
Wakefield Gdns. IG1: Ilf ...4D 18
Wakerfield Cl. RM11: Horn ...3D 24
Wakering Rd. IG11: Bark ...6G 27
  (Barking Northern Relief Rd.)
  IG11: Bark 5G 27
  (Church Rd.)
Wakerings, The *IG11: Bark* ...*5G 27*
  (off Wakering Rd.)
Waldegrave Ct. IG11: Bark ...1D 34
Waldegrave Gdns.
  RM14: Upm 6F 25
Waldegrave Rd. RM8: Dag ...1E 29
Walden Av. RM13: Rain 2H 37
Walden Rd. RM11: Horn 4B 24
Walden Way IG6: Ilf 4A 10
  RM11: Horn
Walfrey Gdns. RM9: Dag 5H 29
Walk, The RM11: Horn 1D 32
Wallace Way RM1: Rom 5D 12
WALLEND 1A 34
Wall End Ct. *E6* *1A 34*
  (off Wall End Rd.)
Wall End Rd. E6 ....6E 27
Wallenger Av. RM2: Rom 1H 23
Wallers Cl. IG8: Wfd G 3D 8
  RM9: Dag 1C 36
Wallingford Ho. *RM3: Rom* ...*3C 14*
  (off Kingsbridge Rd.)
Wallington Rd. IG11: Bark ...5B 20
Wallis Cl. RM13: Rain 6H 23
Walmer Cl. RM7: Mawney ...6B 12
Walnut Cl. IG6: Ilf 2G 19
Walnut Gro. RM12: Horn 6B 24
Walnut Tree Rd. RM8: Dag ...1G 29
Walnut Way RM9: Buck H 1B 8
Walpole Rd. E6 ....6A 26
Walsham Cl. SE28 ....6B 36
Walter Hurford Pde. *E12* ...*3E 27*
  (off Walton Rd.)
Walter Rodney Cl. E6 ......5D 26
Waltham Cl. CM13: Hut 2C 6
Waltham Rd. IG8: Wfd G 3C 8
Walton Gdns. CM13: Hut 1C 6
Walton Rd. E12 ....3E 27
  (not continuous)
  RM5: Col R 4H 11
Wambrook Cl. CM13: Hut 4C 6
Wanderer Dr. IG11: Bark ...3A 36
Wangey Rd. RM6: Chad H 5F 21
Wannock Gdns. IG6: Ilf 4F 9
Wansford Cl. CM14: Bwood ...6B 4

Wansford Rd. IG8: Wfd G 5A 8
Wanstead Gdns. IG4: Ilf ...4B 18
Wanstead La. IG1: Ilf 4B 18
Wanstead Leisure Cen. 4A 18
Wanstead Pk. Av. E12 .....6B 18
Wanstead Pk. Rd. IG1: Ilf ...4B 18
Wantz La. RM13: Rain 4D 38
  (not continuous)
Wantz Rd. RM10: Dag 3B 30
Warden Av. RM5: Col R 2C 12
Ward Gdns. RM3: Hrld W 5B 14
Wards Rd. IG2: Ilf 5H 19
Waremead Rd. IG2: Ilf 3F 19
Warescot Cl. CM15: Bwood ...3D 4
Warescot Rd. CM15: Bwood ...3D 4
WARLEY 2E 17
Warley Av. RM8: Dag 5H 21
Warley Gap
  CM13: Gt War, L War 4D 16
Warley Hill
  CM13: Gt War, War 3D 16
  CM14: War 3D 16
Warley Hill Bus. Pk., The
  CM13: Gt War 3E 17
Warley Mt. CM14: War 1E 17
Warley Rd. CM13: Gt War ...5C 16
  IG5: Ilf 5E 9
  RM14: Gt War, Upm 6G 15
Warleywoods Cres.
  CM14: War 1D 16
Warminster Ho. *RM3: Rom* ...*2D 14*
  (off Redcar Rd.)
Warner Village Cinema
  Dagenham 1C 36
Warren, The E12 ....3C 26
Warren Cl. IG7: Chig 1H 9
Warren Dr. RM12: Horn 3G 31
Warren Dr., The E11 ......5A 18
Warren Farm Cotts.
  RM6: Chad H 2H 21
Warren Rd. E11 ....4A 18
  (not continuous)
  IG6: Ilf 3H 19
Warren Sports Cen. 3H 21
Warren Ter. RM6: Chad H ...2F 21
Warriner Av. RM12: Horn ...1B 32
Warrington Gdns.
  RM11: Horn 4A 24
Warrington Rd. RM8: Dag ...1F 29
Warrington Sq. RM8: Dag ...1F 29
Warrior Sq. E12 ....3E 27
Warwall E6 ....6B 34
Warwick Cl. RM11: Horn 2D 24
Warwick Gdns. IG1: Ilf 6F 19
  RM2: Rom 1A 24
Warwick La. RM13: Rain 3H 39
Warwick Rd. E11 ....3A 18
  E12 ....4C 26
  RM13: Rain 4E 39
Washington Av. E12 ......3D 26
Washington Rd. E6 ....6A 26
Wash Rd. CM13: Hut, Mount ...2D 6
Waterbeach Rd. RM9: Dag ...5E 29
Water La. IG3: Ilf 2A 28
Waterloo Gdns. RM7: Rom ...4D 22
Waterloo Rd. CM14: Bwood ...4E 5
  E6 ....6A 26
  IG6: Ilf 6G 9
  RM7: Rom, Rush G 3E 23
Watermans RM1: Rom 3F 23
Waters Gdns. RM10: Dag 4A 30
Waterside Cl. IG11: Bark ...3C 28
  RM3: Hrld W 4E 15
Watersmeet Way SE28 ......6A 36
Water Tower Cl.
  CM14: Gt War 2E 17
Wates Way CM15: Bwood 4F 5
Watford Ho. *RM3: Rom* *2D 14*
  (off Redruth Rd.)
Watson Av. E6 ....6E 27
Watson Gdns. RM3: Hrld W ...6B 14
Waverley Cl. E18 ....5A 8
Waverley Cres. RM1: Rom ...4A 14
Waverley Gdns. IG6: Ilf ...6G 9
  IG11: Bark 2E 35
Waverley Rd. E18 ....5A 8
  RM13: Rain 4D 38
Waycross Rd. RM14: Upm ...3A 40
Wayside Av. RM13: Rain 1B 32
Wayside Cl. RM1: Rom 1F 23
Wayside Commercial Cen.
  IG11: Bark 1F 35
Wayside Gdns. RM10: Dag ...4A 30
Wayside M. IG2: Ilf 3E 19
Weald Cl. CM14: Bwood 6C 4

Weald Country Pk. 3A 4
Weald Pk. Way CM14: S Weald ...6A 4
Weald Rd. CM14: S Weald ...5A 4
Weald Way RM7: Rom 4B 22
Weaver Cl. E6 ....6B 34
Webb Ho. *RM10: Dag* *2A 30*
  (off Kershaw Rd.)
Webbscroft Rd. RM10: Dag ...3B 30
Webster Cl. RM12: Horn 2B 32
Wedderburn Rd. IG11: Bark ...1E 35
Wedlake Cl. RM11: Horn 6C 24
Wedmore Av. IG5: Ilf 5E 9
Wednesbury Gdns.
  RM3: Rom 4D 14
Wednesbury Grn. RM3: Rom ...4D 14
Wednesbury Rd. RM3: Rom ...4D 14
Well Cott. Cl. E11 ....4A 18
Wellesley Rd. CM14: Bwood ...4E 5
  IG1: Ilf 1F 27
Wellingborough Ho.
  RM3: Rom *2D 14*
  (off Redruth Rd.)
Wellington Cl. RM10: Dag ...6C 30
Wellington Dr. RM10: Dag ...6C 30
Wellington Ho. RM2: Rom ...2A 24
Wellington Av.
  RM4: Have B 1C 12
Wellington Pl. CM14: War ...2E 17
Wellington Rd. E6 ....1A 34
Wellington St. IG11: Bark ...1C 34
Wells Gdns. IG1: Ilf 5C 18
  RM10: Dag 4B 30
  RM13: Rain 5F 31
Wells Ho. *IG11: Bark* *6C 28*
  (off Margaret Bondfield Av.)
Wellstead Rd. E6 ....2A 34
Wellwood Rd. IG3: Ilf 6C 20
Wendover Gdns. CM13: Bwood ...5B 6
Wendover Way RM12: Horn ...4A 32
Wenham Gdns. CM13: Hut ...2C 6
Wennington Rd.
  RM13: Rain, Wenn 4C 38
Wensley Cl. RM5: Col R 2A 12
Wensleydale Av. IG5: Ilf ...6C 8
Wentworth Cl. SE28 ......6B 36
Wentworth Rd. E12 ....3B 26
Wentworth Way RM13: Rain ...3D 38
Werneth Hall Rd. IG5: Ilf ...1D 18
Wessex Cl. IG3: Ilf 4A 20
West Bank IG11: Bark 1B 34
Westbourne Dr.
  CM14: Bwood 1B 16
Westbury Ct. *IG11: Bark* ...*1D 34*
  (off Westbury Rd.)
Westbury Dr. CM14: Bwood ...5E 5
Westbury Rd. CM14: Bwood ...5E 5
  E7 ....5A 26
  IG1: Ilf 1E 27
  IG11: Bark 1D 34
Westbury Ter. E7 ....5A 26
  RM14: Upm 5A 40
West Cl. RM13: Rain 4D 38
W. Dene Dr. RM3: Rom 2B 14
Western Av. CM14: Bwood ...4E 5
  RM2: Rom 6A 14
  RM10: Dag 5C 30
Western Ct. *RM1: Rom* *3E 23*
  (off Chandlers Way)
Western Gdns. CM14: Bwood ...5E 5
Western Pathway
  RM12: Horn 6H 31
  RM13: Rain 6H 31
Western Rd. CM14: Bwood ...5E 5
  RM1: Rom 3E 23
Westernville Gdns. IG2: Ilf ...5G 19
Westfield Gdns. RM6: Chad H ...4E 21
Westfield Pk. Dr. IG8: Wfd G ...3C 8
Westfield Rd. RM9: Dag 5G 29
West Gro. IG8: Wfd G 3A 8
Westland Av. RM11: Horn ...6C 24
Westlyn Cl. RM13: Rain 4E 39
W. Malling Way RM12: Horn ...4A 32
Westmede IG7: Chig 3G 9
Westminster Cl. IG6: Ilf ...6H 9
Westminster Gdns. IG6: Ilf ...6H 9
  IG11: Bark 2E 35
Westmoreland Av.
  RM11: Horn 3A 24
Westmorland Cl. E12 ......1B 26
Weston Cl. CM13: Hut 3C 6
Westone Mans. *IG11: Bark* ...*6B 28*
  (off Upney La.)
Weston Grn. RM9: Dag 3H 29
Weston Rd. RM9: Dag 3G 29
Weston St. RM6: Chad H 3F 21

West Pk. Hill CM14: Bwood 6C 4
West Rd. RM6: Chad H 4F 21
   RM7: Rush G 5D 22
Westrow Dr. IG11: Bark 4C 28
Westrow Gdns. IG3: Ilf 1B 28
Westview Cl. RM13: Rain 3E 39
Westview Dr. IG8: Wfd G 6B 8
West Way CM14: Bwood 6C 4
Westwood Av. CM14: Bwood . . .1C 16
Westwood Rd. IG3: Ilf 6B 20
Weyland Rd. RM8: Dag 2H 29
Weymouth Cl. E6 . . . . .6B 34
Whalebone Av. RM6: Chad H . .4H 21
Whalebone Gro.
   RM6: Chad H 4H 21
Whalebone La. Nth.
   RM6: Chad H, Col R 4G 11
Whalebone La. Sth.
   RM6: Chad H, Dag 5H 21
   RM8: Dag 5H 21
Wharf Rd. CM14: Bwood 6E 5
Wheatfields CM14: War 1E 17
   E6 . . . . .6B 34
Wheatley Cl. RM11: Horn 3B 24
Wheatley Mans. IG11: Bark 6C 28
                (off Bevan Av.)
Wheatsheaf Rd. RM1: Rom 4F 23
Wheeler Cl. IG8: Wfd G 3D 8
Wheelers Cross IG11: Bark 2D 34
Wheel Farm Dr. RM10: Dag 2C 30
Whimbrel Cl. SE28 . . . . .6A 36
Whistler M. RM8: Dag 4D 28
       (off Fitzstephen Rd.)
Whitchurch Rd. RM3: Rom 1B 14
Whitebarn La. RM10: Dag 1E 37
White Gdns. RM10: Dag 5A 30
White Gates RM12: Horn 1A 32
White Hart La. CM14: Bwood . . .5E 5
   RM7: Col R, Mawney 5A 12
White Horse Rd. E6 . . . . .3A 34
Whitelands Way RM3: Hrld W . .5B 14
White Lyons Rd. CM14: Bwood . .5E 5
Whites Av. IG2: Ilf 4A 20
Whitethorn Gdns.
   RM11: Horn 4A 24
Whitfield Ct. IG1: Ilf 5D 18
Whitfield Rd. E6 . . . . .6A 26
Whiting Av. IG11: Bark 6F 27
Whitings IG2: Ilf 3A 20
Whitings Way E6 . . . . .5A 34
Whitmore Av. RM3: Hrld W 6C 14
Whittaker Rd. E6 . . . . .6A 26
Whitta Rd. E12 . . . . .3B 26
Whittington Rd. CM13: Hut 2C 6
Whitworth Cen., The
   RM3: Rom 2A 14
Whybridge Cl. RM13: Rain 1B 38
Whyteville Rd. E7 . . . . .5A 26
Wickets Way IG6: Ilf 3B 10
Wickfields IG7: Chig 3H 9
Wickford Cl. RM3: Rom 2D 14
Wickford Dr. RM3: Rom 2D 14
Wid Cl. CM13: Hut 1D 6
Widecombe Cl. RM3: Rom 5B 14
Widecombe Gdns. IG4: Ilf 2C 18
Widworthy Hayes CM13: Hut . . .4B 6
Wigley Bush La.
   CM14: Bwood, S Weald 5A 4
Wigram Rd. E11 . . . . .4A 18
Wigton Rd. RM3: Rom 1C 14
Wigton Way RM3: Rom 1C 14
Wilfred Av. RM13: Rain 5C 38

Wilkes Rd. CM13: Hut 1D 6
William Cl. RM5: Col R 5C 12
William Hunter Way
   CM14: Bwood 5E 5
William Pike Ho. RM7: Rom . . .4D 22
      (off Waterloo Gdns.)
William St. IG11: Bark 6G 27
Willingale Cl. CM13: Hut 2E 7
   IG8: Wfd G 3A 8
Willoughby Dr. RM13: Rain 6E 31
Willow Cl. CM13: Hut 2B 6
   RM12: Horn 2H 31
Willowdene CM15: Pil H 1B 4
Willowdene Cl. CM14: War 1E 17
Willowherb Path RM3: Rom . . .4A 14
Willow Pde. RM14: Upm 4A 40
Willow Rd. E12 . . . . .2D 26
   RM6: Chad H 4G 21
Willows, The E6 . . . . .6D 26
Willow St. RM7: Rom 2C 22
Willow Wlk. IG1: Ilf 1F 27
   RM14: Upm 4A 40
Willow Way RM3: Hrld W 3F 15
         (not continuous)
Will Perrin Ct. RM13: Rain 1C 38
Wilmington Gdns. IG11: Bark . .5H 27
Wilmot Grn. CM13: Gt War 3E 17
Wilmslow Rd. RM3: Rom 2C 14
      (off Chudleigh Rd.)
Wilson Rd. IG1: Ilf 5D 18
Wilsons Cnr. CM14: Bwood 5F 5
           (off High St.)
Wilthorne Gdns. RM10: Dag . . .6B 30
Wilton Dr. RM5: Col R 4C 12
Wiltshire Av. RM11: Horn 2D 24
Wiltshire Ct. IG1: Ilf 5G 27
Wincanton Gdns. IG6: Ilf 1F 19
Wincanton Rd. RM3: Rom 1B 14
Winchester Av. RM14: Upm 4B 40
Winchester Rd. IG11: Bark 6C 28
      (off Keir Hardie Way)
Winchester Rd. IG1: Ilf 2H 27
Windermere Av. RM12: Horn . . .4G 31
Windermere Gdns. IG4: Ilf 3C 18
Winding Way RM8: Dag 2E 29
Windmill Ct. RM14: Upm 1E 33
Windsor Rd. CM15: Pil H 2D 4
   E7 . . . . .4A 26
   IG1: Ilf 3F 27
   RM8: Dag 2G 29
   RM11: Horn 5A 24
Windy Hill CM13: Hut 4C 6
Wingate Rd. IG1: Ilf 4F 27
Wingfield Cl. CM13: Bwood 6A 6
Wingfield Gdns. RM14: Upm . . .2A 40
Wingletye La. RM11: Horn 2D 24
Wingrave Cres.
   CM14: Bwood 1A 16
Wingrove Ct. RM7: Rom 3C 22
Wing Way CM14: Bwood 4E 5
Winifred Av. RM12: Horn 3B 32
Winifred Dell Ho.
   CM13: Gt War 3E 17
Winifred Rd. RM8: Dag 1G 29
Winifred Whittington Ho.
   RM13: Rain 5D 38
Winmill Rd. RM8: Dag 2H 29
Winningales Ct. IG5: Ilf 6C 8
WINSOR PARK 5B 34
Winsor Ter. E6 . . . . .5A 34
Winstead Gdns. RM10: Dag . . .4C 30
Winston Cl. RM7: Mawney 2B 22
Winston Way IG1: Ilf 2F 27

Winterbourne Rd. RM8: Dag . . .1E 29
Wisdons Cl. RM10: Dag 6B 22
Wistaria Cl. CM15: Pil H 1E 5
Wisteria Cl. IG1: Ilf 1F 27
Witham Rd. RM2: Rom 2H 23
   RM10: Dag 4A 30
Witherings, The
   RM11: Horn 3C 24
Wittering Wlk. RM12: Horn 5A 32
Wivenhoe Rd. IG11: Bark 2G 35
Wix Rd. RM9: Dag 1B 36
Woburn Av. RM12: Horn 3G 31
Woburn Cl. SE28 . . . . .6B 36
Wolferton Rd. E12 . . . . .3D 26
Wolseley Rd. RM7: Rush G 5D 22
Wolsey Av. E6 . . . . .3A 34
Wolsey Gdns. IG6: Ilf 3F 9
Wolverton Ho. RM3: Rom 2C 14
       (off Chudleigh Rd.)
Woodbridge Cl. RM3: Rom 1B 14
Woodbridge Ct. IG8: Wfd G 4C 8
Woodbridge La. RM3: Rom 1B 14
Woodbridge Rd. IG11: Bark 4B 28
Woodcote Av. RM12: Horn 3G 31
Woodcutters Cl. RM11: Horn . . .2B 24
Woodfield Dr. RM2: Rom 2G 23
Woodfield Way RM12: Horn 6B 24
Woodfines, The RM11: Horn . . .4B 24
WOODFORD 3A 8
Woodford Av. IG2: Ilf 3D 18
   IG4: Ilf, Wfd G 1B 18
WOODFORD BRIDGE 3C 8
Woodford Bri. Rd. IG4: Ilf 1B 18
Woodford Station (Tube) 3A 8
Woodford Trad. Est.
   IG8: Wfd G 6B 8
WOODFORD WELLS 1A 8
Woodgrange Park Station (Rail)
              . . . . . .4B 26
Woodhall Cres. RM11: Horn . . .5D 24
Woodhaven Gdns. IG6: Ilf 2G 19
Woodhouse Gro. E12 . . . . .5C 26
Woodland Av. CM13: Hut 1C 6
   E12 . . . . .2C 26
Woodland Cl. CM13: Hut 1C 6
Woodlands Av. E11 . . . . .6A 18
   RM6: Chad H 4G 21
   RM11: Horn 3B 24
Woodlands Rd. IG1: Ilf 2G 27
   RM1: Rom 1F 23
   RM3: Hrld W 5E 15
Wood La. RM8: Dag 3E 29
   RM9: Dag 3E 29
   RM10: Dag 1A 30
   RM11: Horn 4G 31
Woodman Path IG6: Ilf 3A 10
Woodman Rd. CM14: War 2E 17
Woodrush Way RM6: Chad H . . .2F 21
Woodshire Rd. RM10: Dag 2B 30
Woodside Cl. CM13: Hut 1D 6
   RM13: Rain 4E 39
Woodside Ct. E12 . . . . .6A 18
Woodside Av. RM3: Rom 2F 15
Woodstock Gdns. IG3: Ilf 1C 28
Woodstock Rd. E7 . . . . .6A 26
Woodville Gdns. IG6: Ilf 1F 19
Woodville Rd. E18 . . . . .6A 8
Woodward Gdns. RM9: Dag . . .6E 29
Woodward Rd. RM9: Dag 6D 28
Woodway CM13: Hut 4A 6
   CM15: Hut, Shenf 4A 6
Woolhampton Way IG7: Chig . . .1D 10

Woolwich Mnr. Way E6 . . . . . . .4A 34
Wootton Cl. RM11: Horn 3B 24
Worcester Av. RM14: Upm 5B 40
Worcester Cres. IG8: Wfd G 1A 8
Worcester Gdns. IG1: Ilf 5C 18
Worcester Rd. E12 . . . . .3D 26
Wordsworth Av. E12 . . . . .6C 26
Wordsworth Ct. RM3: Rom 5A 14
Worrin Cl. CM15: Shenf 4H 5
Worrin Rd. CM15: Shenf 5H 5
Wortley Rd. E6 . . . . .6B 26
Wray Av. IG5: Ilf 1E 19
Wray Cl. RM11: Horn 5A 24
Wren Gdns. RM9: Dag 4F 29
   RM12: Horn 6F 23
Wren Pl. CM14: Bwood 6F 5
Wren Rd. RM9: Dag 4F 29
Wrexham Rd. RM3: Rom 1B 14
Wrights Cl. RM10: Dag 3B 30
Wrington Ho. RM3: Rom 2D 14
        (off Redruth Rd.)
Writtle Wlk. RM13: Rain 1A 38
Wroxall Rd. RM9: Dag 5E 29
Wroxham Rd. SE28 . . . . .6B 36
Wroxham Way IG6: Ilf 5F 9
Wych Elm Cl. RM11: Horn 5E 25
Wych Elm Rd. RM11: Horn 4E 25
Wychwood Gdns. IG5: Ilf 2D 18
Wycombe Rd. IG2: Ilf 3D 18
Wyfields IG5: Ilf 5F 9
Wyhill Wlk. RM10: Dag 5C 30
Wykeham Av. RM9: Dag 5E 29
   RM11: Horn 4B 24
Wykeham Grn. RM9: Dag 5E 29
Wymans Way E7 . . . . .3A 26
Wymark Ct. RM13: Rain 2C 38
Wyndham Rd. E6 . . . . .6B 26
Wyndale Cl. IG8: Wfd G 5B 8
Wynndale Rd. E18 . . . . .4A 8
Wythenshawe Rd. RM10: Dag . . .2A 30

Yale Way RM12: Horn 3G 31
Yellowpine Way IG7: Chig 1D 10
Yelverton Cl. RM3: Rom 5B 14
Yeoman Cl. E6 . . . . .6B 34
Yeoman Way IG6: Ilf 3G 9
Yevele Way RM11: Horn 5C 24
Yew Tree Cl. CM13: Hut 2B 6
Yew Tree Gdns. RM6: Chad H . .3G 21
   RM7: Rom 3D 22
Yew Tree Lodge RM7: Rom 3D 22
      (off Yew Tree Gdns.)
York Cl. CM15: Shenf 3H 5
York M. IG1: Ilf 2E 27
York Pl. IG1: Ilf 1E 27
   RM10: Dag 5C 30
York Rd. CM15: Shenf 3H 5
   IG1: Ilf 2E 27
   RM13: Rain 6D 30
Youngs Rd. IG2: Ilf 3H 19
Yoxley App. IG2: Ilf 4G 19
Yoxley Dr. IG2: Ilf 4G 19